Cat. 11.16

TWAYNE'S WORLD AUTHORS SERIES
A Survey of the World's Literature

CANADA

Joseph Jones, University of Texas, Austin

EDITOR

Sinclair Ross

TWAS 504

SINCLAIR ROSS

By LORRAINE McMULLEN

University of Ottawa

TWAYNE PUBLISHERS
A DIVISION OF G. K. HALL & CO., BOSTON

813.5̄2
R826 M
1979

Library of Congress Cataloging in Publication Data

McMullen, Lorraine.
Sinclair Ross.

(Twayne's world authors series ; TWAS 504:
Canada)
Bibliography: p. 154–57
Includes index.
1. Ross, Sinclair.
2. Authors, Canadian—20th century—Biography.
PR9199.R599Z77   813'.5'2 [B]   78-27671
ISBN 0-8057-6385-6

For My Mother

Contents

About the Author

Lorraine McMullen is a professor at University of Ottawa and has been visiting professor at the special Summer Institute of English Studies, Concordia University, Montreal. Her literary interests include late nineteenth and twentieth century literature as well as Canadian literature. She has written extensively on Canadian literature. Her books include *An Introduction to the Aesthetic Movement in English Literature, Selected Stories of E. W. Thomson, The Lampman Symposium,* and *Twentieth-Century Essays on Confederation Literature.*

Preface

Sinclair Ross is a key figure in Canadian prairie fiction. His stories of the dust bowl and depression prairie and his novels of the small, puritanical prairie towns are at the heart of the exploration of man and landscape in the Canadian West.

In "The Prairie: A State of Mind," Henry Kreisel describes the two opposing reactions of man to the prairie: "Man, the giant-conqueror, and man, the insignificant dwarf always threatened by defeat, form the two polarities of the state of mind produced by the sheer physical fact of the prairie."[1] Of these two polarities, Ross most often exemplifies the sense of confinement and repression, of man's insignificance, whether in the claustrophobic atmosphere of the town or in the unlimited space of the prairie. Although some of Ross's farmers continue the heroic dream of "man, the giant-conqueror," which is at the center of Frederick Philip Grove's prairie fiction, for most the land proves a fickle mistress—their years of servitude to her most often ending in failure and despair.

In the chronology of prairie fiction writers, Ross follows early realists such as Frederick Philip Grove, and precedes the generation of Margaret Laurence, Robert Kroetsch, and Rudy Wiebe. Ross's protagonists are unlike the heroic patriarchal figures in the new land which Grove depicts. Whether exploring town or prairie, Ross creates a portrait of the tensions and suppressed passions of men and women of an austere land and puritanical religion. His mythic prairie town is much like Margaret Laurence's fictional town of Manawaka, repressive, puritanical, and a cultural desert.

In any assessment of his significance as a writer, Ross's role in the development of prairie fiction must be noted. Equally relevant, however, is a consideration of his themes. Ross's most persistent themes, the problems of the artist and the search for a son, place him in the mainstream of Canadian writing. Alienation, failure of communication, the problem of the imagination—and through all, a search for meaning in an incomprehensible universe—these are major concerns of our century to which Ross gives voice in his fiction.

Finally, one must consider Ross's masterly control of form. His metaphoric use of landscape to mirror the psychic lives of his characters, his taut, economical, rhythmic prose, the complex interweaving of action, character, and landscape—all contribute to the impact of his art. For all these reasons, Sinclair Ross is a figure of major importance in Canadian literature, despite the relatively small body of work he has published.

This critical study begins with a chapter outlining aspects of Ross's life and background relevant to his writing. It is followed by chapters on the short stories and on each novel, a chapter presenting an overall conception of Ross's fictional world and his ironic stance, and a brief conclusion.

I deal at some length with Ross's short stories since the techniques he develops and the perception of the world he demonstrates in the early stories give an indication of the direction in which his fiction continues. Further, many of Ross's stories concerning the impact of landscape on the individual remain among his finest works. They deserve a central place in a study of his works.

Acknowledgments

I am especially grateful to Sinclair Ross for his cooperation and for the many pleasant sunny afternoons we spent on the Costa del Sol in March 1977 discussing his life and writing.

I wish also to express my appreciation to my colleagues: Laurence Ricou, University of Lethbridge, who made many helpful suggestions, and Sandra Djwa, Simon Fraser University, with whom I discussed several aspects of this study. Errors or omissions are, of course, my own.

I am happy to acknowledge my appreciation to the University of Ottawa for the sabbatical leave during which I completed my research and to the Canada Council for the research grant to support it.

Passages from *As For Me and My House, Whir of Gold, Sawbones Memorial,* and *The Lamp at Noon and Other Stories* by Sinclair Ross reprinted by permission of The Canadian Publishers, McClelland and Stewart Limited, Toronto, Canada, to whom I express my thanks.

Chronology

1908   James Sinclair Ross born January 22 to Peter Ross and Catherine Foster Fraser Ross on a homestead in northern Saskatchewan, twelve miles from Shellbrooke and twenty-five miles from Prince Albert.

1924   Completed grade eleven at the high school at Indian Head, Sask. Began working for the Union Bank of Canada (which was later absorbed by The Royal Bank of Canada) at Abbey, Sask.

1928   Transferred by The Royal Bank of Canada to Lancer, Sask. on April 7, 1928.

1929   Transferred by the bank to Arcola, Sask. on June 6, 1929.

1933   Transferred by the bank to Winnipeg, Manitoba in April, 1933.

1934   First story, "No Other Way" won third prize of twenty pounds in Nash's Short Story Competition. The story was published in *Nash's Pall-Mall* October 1934.

1935   "A Field of Wheat" published in *Queen's Quarterly* XLII, 1 (Spring, 1935). This was the first of twelve stories published in *Queen's Quarterly*.

1941   *As For Me and My House* published by Reynal and Hitchcock, New York.

1942   Joined the Canadian Army and was sent overseas with the Ordnance Corps. Served with Army Headquarters, London, England until 1946.

1946   Returned to Winnipeg, Canada early in the year. Was demobilized from the army and returned to The Royal Bank of Canada. In April was transferred by the bank to its headquarters in Montreal.

1957   *As For Me and My House* published in New Canadian Library edition, McClelland and Stewart, Toronto.

1958   *The Well* published by Macmillan, Toronto.

1968   January 31, 1968 retired from The Royal Bank of Canada. March 1968 moved to Athens, Greece, where he lived for three years. *The Lamp at Noon and Other Stories*, a collection of previously published stories, published in New Canadian Library edition, McClelland and Stewart, Toronto.

1970   *Whir of Gold* published by McClelland and Stewart, Toronto.

1971   March 1971 moved to Barcelona, Spain.

1973   Moved from Barcelona to Malaga, Spain.

1974   *Sawbones Memorial* published by McClelland and Stewart, Toronto.

1978   *Sawbones Memorial* published in New Canadian Library edition, McClelland and Stewart, Toronto.

1978   *As For Me and My House* published by University of Nebraska Press, Lincoln, Nebraska.

CHAPTER 1

Introduction

I *Biographical Notes*

JAMES Sinclair Ross was born January 22, 1908 on a homestead in northern Saskatchewan, twelve miles from Shellbrooke and twenty-five miles from Prince Albert. He was the third child and second son of Catherine Foster Fraser and Peter Ross. The elder boy, Stuart, had been born seven years earlier, and the daughter, Euphemia, ten years earlier. Peter, Sinclair Ross's father, had been born in 1868 on a farm near Owen Sound, Ontario, of parents who had come from the Shetland Islands to settle in Canada. He went West as a young man, and was working in Prince Albert with a dray and team when he met and married Catherine Foster Fraser in 1897. Subsequently, they took up the homestead of one hundred and sixty acres where Sinclair Ross was born.

Catherine Foster Fraser was born in Edinburgh in 1876. Her father, John Foster Fraser, had studied for the ministry at the University of Edinburgh and, according to his daughter, had taught theology at Oberlin College, Ohio before ordination. Here he had come under the influence of the Unitarian ideas of Theodore Parker. After completing his studies at Edinburgh University he took up his calling as a Unitarian minister. He died suddenly at the age of twenty-nine, leaving a wife and five children. His widow subsequently married Thomas Holmes and came with him to Prince Albert where he had obtained a job with the Canadian Pacific Railway. Three of the five children, Catherine and her two brothers, came to Canada with their mother and stepfather. The other daughter had died in childhood. The eldest son, John Foster Fraser, (later Sir John Foster Fraser), remained in Britain and later acquired a reputation as journalist and travel writer. Sinclair Ross had some slight contact with this uncle, who died in 1936.

When Jimmy, as Sinclair Ross's family called him, was three years of age, his parents separated. An attempted reconciliation failed, and they separated permanently when he was six or seven. Jimmy remained with his mother and the two older children with his father. Ross does not seem to have been in touch with his father since this time, although he has been in communication with his sister, Euphemia, who married, settled on a farm in Saskatchewan and died in 1969; and with his brother, Stuart, now living in Detroit. Ross recalls his mother saying that his father had suffered a marked personality change as the result of serious injuries incurred in an accident caused by a runaway horse; she blamed this accident for the difficulties which led to their separation. Ross, himself, dimly remembers as a small child seeing his father learning to walk again after the accident, using a chair as a walker.

After Mrs. Ross left her husband, she supported herself and her young son by working on various farms as a housekeeper. As he grew older Jimmy helped with the farm chores. When at the age of sixteen he completed high school at Indian Head in 1924, he obtained employment with The Union Bank of Canada (later taken over by The Royal Bank of Canada) at Abbey, Saskatchewan, where he remained for four years. In 1928 he was transferred to Lancer, Saskatchewan and in 1929 to Arcola, Saskatchewan. In 1933 he was moved to Winnipeg where, apart from a period of four years when he enlisted in the Canadian Army and went overseas with the Ordnance Corps, he remained until 1946. The army found him too underweight for duty on the continent, so he spent most of his army years in London, England. A few months after his return in 1946 he was transferred by the Royal Bank to Montreal, where he remained until his retirement in 1968. He then moved to Greece where he lived for three years and in March 1971 to Spain—first to Barcelona and then to Malaga—where he now resides.

II *Background*

Sinclair Ross's mother was the single most profound influence in his life. She was a voracious reader who encouraged her son to read from his earliest years. Mrs. Ross was a great admirer of Sir Walter Scott and Charles Dickens. Ross recalls when as a youngster, winning a copy of Scott's *Ivanhoe* at school, he was admonished by his mother as he hurried through his reading of the book, that such a great writer should be read more slowly and savored appreciatively.[1] He speaks of his mother as a determined woman, "a fighter," who worked very hard to give him an education. To give one example, she bought him a horse to ride to school when during harvest or other busy times on the farm a horse could not be spared from the field; such was her determination that her son would have proper schooling. This horse, "Lady," was the prototype for young Peter McAlpine's Isabel, in "The Outlaw" and *Whir of Gold*. The presence of his mother's strong will made her son a fighter also; apparently living with such a woman called forth an equal combativeness on his part. His strong determination stood Ross in good stead, for he persisted in his writing over many years with little encouragement.

Ross supported his mother from the time he started to work at sixteen. She lived with him in the small towns where he was posted with the bank, and also in Winnipeg, and remained in his Winnipeg apartment while he was overseas. When Ross was transferred to Montreal, his mother remained in the West, living for a time with her daughter, then with other families, and finally in a nursing home. Ross continued to accept responsibility for his mother until her death in 1957. Thus, although Sinclair Ross never married, he has had family responsibilities of a kind which would tend to discourage thoughts of giving up regular employment to devote full time to writing.

Ross relates that his mother was very conscious of her background. She was the daughter of a clergyman of upper class ancestry, a man with a University of Edinburgh education and possessor of an extensive library. As a result, she always felt herself somewhat superior to other homesteaders and farmers. Ross says that as he grew older he often found her pride in her family ridiculous and maddening, but he understands now that it helped her through some bad times. "I may be working for you and taking your orders," she was in effect saying, "but I'm better born."

Ross was brought up by his mother as a Unitarian. Again, being a Unitarian rather than a Presbyterian, his mother did not fit the small prairie town stereotype. Ross remembers that as a child he learned at school that Christ was Divine, whereas his mother had taught him that Christ was a man, albeit a remarkable one. When he asked his mother for clarification of these two opposing views, she admonished him to remember that the essential idea was to be Christlike in one's actions. Mrs. Ross was always to stress love of neighbor. When the Ku Klux Klan began to make headway in small prairie communities, she courageously spoke out against it, although in general the town was rallying to the Klan's support.

Ross recalls an amusing incident when the business community in their small town supported the Klan, although there was a single Roman Catholic in the town, the milkman. The milkman had the last laugh when businessmen accustomed to using his field for a golf course found a "No Trespassing" sign on the gate. Sinclair Ross himself claims at the present time to be an agnostic. Doubtless because of his mother's training and example he retains a strong sense of responsibility and a generally compassionate attitude.

Ross recalls that as a child he was interested in writing; he was probably about ten years of age when he began trying to express himself through writing. He received no particular encouragement from teachers, or even from his mother, although she always encouraged reading. However, Mrs. Ross was pleased with her son's success. She particularly liked stories such as "Circus in Town" and "A Day with Pegasus," disliking "The Painted Door" and As For Me and My House.

Ross first submitted a story for publication at age sixteen. It was rejected and he waited five years before trying again.[2] His first published story was "No Other Way" which won third prize of twenty pounds in Nash's Short Story Competition for previously unpublished writers. The story appeared in Nash's-Pall Mall, October 1934. At this time Ross was twenty-six years of age. He is quoted in Nash's-Pall Mall as saying at this time that he had written two novels, "failures, which publishers write me are interesting and compelling, but of small commercial possibilities. I am now starting to work on short stories, hoping gradually to build up a better technique without the cramping grind that writing a novel after office hours demands."[3] Nash's award was a significant achievement since there were more than eight thousand entries. The judges were Somerset Maugham, Desmond MacCarthy, and Rebecca West. According to the magazine Ross had written the story three years earlier and rewritten it twice. He was to publish seven stories in the next five years, all in Queen's Quarterly.

When he obtained his first job at sixteen Ross bought a piano and began music lessons, continuing to study the piano for several years. Music plays an important role in the lives of many of his protagonists. Musical structure, too, has had an influence on Ross's craft, especially apparent in As For Me and My House and Sawbones Memorial. Rhythm and intonation are always important to his writing; many of the slight revisions Ross makes in his stories when they are reprinted are designed to improve the rhythm of the sentences.

The young Ross was also interested in painting. As a youth he experimented with oils, but did not find painting a satisfactory medium of expression. However, the eye of the painter as well as the ear of the musician has had its effect on his writing. Thirteen-year-old Peter in "The Outlaw," for example, views the landscape with a painter's eye as he gallops across the prairie on his horse, Isabel: "And I too, responsive to her bidding, was aware as never before of its austere, unrelenting beauty. There were the white fields and the blue, metallic sky; the little splashes here and there of yellow strawstack, luminous and clear as drops of gum on fresh pine lumber; the scattered farmsteads brave and wistful in their isolation; the gleam of sun and snow."[4]

In the small Saskatchewan towns where Ross and his mother lived the nine years from 1924 to 1933, Ross participated in the life of the community, as would be expected of a bank employee. He taught Sunday School, played the organ at church, and attended church services, but never became a member of the Presbyterian or United Church he attended. He relates that he was never too enthusiastic about playing the organ at funerals, but his attempts to avoid this, because of his work at the bank, were foiled by community-minded bank managers who readily acceded to requests that he be permitted time from work for funerals.

Most of Ross's early stories which deal with the homestead and with bleak dust bowl days were published between 1933, the year he moved to Winnipeg, and 1942, when he joined the army. Interestingly, Winnipeg was never a setting for any of his stories although he spent nine years there. In published excerpts of letters written in 1970, Ross comments:

. . . I couldn't write three hundred words on the influence of Manitoba on my work, much less three thousand, for the simple reason that it had no influence whatsoever. If I have any claim to be considered a "writer" it must be based on the stories in *The Lamp at Noon* and *As For Me and My House*, and they are, as you know, one hundred per cent Saskatchewan. True, I wrote them while in Winnipeg, but I was looking back, and drew on Manitoba not at all. If I had written them in London or Timbuctoo they would have come out exactly the same.[5]

Ross wrote and destroyed two novels before *As For Me and My House* was published by Reynal and Hitchcock, New York, in 1941. A few copies of the novel were imported for the Canadian market by McClelland and Stewart, but in all, only a few hundred copies were sold. Not until publication of the paperback edition in 1957 did the novel achieve the recognition it deserved. Ross recalls the incident in Saskatchewan which was to be the basis for his novel. A minister told Ross he thought a college education to study for the ministry could be arranged for him. Ross, not at all tempted to pursue the matter, later began to wonder what would happen if a young man who was not a believer were to accept such an arrangement, solely to obtain an education. The title of the novel which resulted, and the motto, "As for Me and My House We Will Serve the Lord," which appears on the wall of a prairie farmhouse parlor in "Cornet at Night," derive from Ross's actual observation of this motto on the wall of a minister's parlor. Ross says that he was really not aware of where in the Bible this quotation appears. His portrayal of the minister and his wife in the novel as largely out of step with the community was partly the result of his acquaintance with such a couple, who had a tendency to antagonize their parishioners in relatively innocuous ways.

Ross's own religious training as a Unitarian was broader than the Protestantism he attributes to his fictional townspeople, who are generally narrow, obsessed with the work ethic, and concerned with appearances. There are certainly evidences of a puritanical bias in the plot structure of his stories and novels, however, and in the treatment of characters and in their fates. Retributive justice is often apparent, and sexual transgression generally receives quick and harsh punishment.

During his term in the army Ross advanced from private to sergeant. After basic training he was posted to the Ordnance Corps and soon sent to Headquarters in London, England. Since Headquarters staff did not live in barracks for fear that a direct hit would decimate the center, Ross lived in his own room in a small bed and breakfast hotel near Russell Square, and was free to enjoy London in his leisure time. Despite bombing raids and the buzz bombs of the latter days of the war, theaters tended to ignore air raid alarms and carry on. For Ross the opportunity to enjoy London theaters and symphonies was marvellous. Having no family responsibilities for the first time gave him a great sense of freedom. He looks back to his London years as the happiest time of his life.

In October 1946, shortly after rejoining the Royal Bank at Winnipeg, Ross was transferred to Montreal head office where he remained until his retirement on January 31, 1968. For his last nine or ten years with the bank, he worked in the advertising department. While in Montreal, he wrote *The Well* (1958), which he had hoped would prove more popular than his earlier novel. It was not, however, a success. During the war he had worked on a novel about a Canadian soldier from Manitoba, but was not satisfied with it and destroyed the manuscript. He did publish two stories relating experiences of Canadian soldiers, "Barrack Room Fiddle Tune" and "Jug and Bottle," the former set in Canada and the latter in England. While in Montreal he published three more stories with Saskatchewan backgrounds. During his years in this city, Ross lived quietly in an apartment within walking distance of his office. Few of his associates at the bank realized that he was a writer. Although he met, very briefly, several Canadian writers in Montreal, including Hugh MacLennan and Ralph Gustafson, he never became an acquaintance of any of them nor a participant in any literary group. He met the Canadian expatriate writer Mavis Gallant several times on her visits to Montreal. In later years in Montreal Ross worked on *Whir of Gold* which was completed after his retirement. The story "Spike" appeared in French translation in *Liberté* the year after his retirement.

Health was a major factor in Ross's decision to live in the Mediterranean area. Ross has cosmopolitan interests. He is interested in languages, reads French and Spanish writers in the original—speaks French and Spanish—and has a considerable knowledge of Greek (in which he has to first "think" before he speaks). One of the reasons he left Athens for Spain was his realization that he would never feel completely at home in the finer points of the Greek language, a difficult language. In Spanish Ross appears quite fluent. The last few years he has become interested in South American novelists, evincing special admiration for the Colombian, Garcia Marquez, and the Peruvian, Vargas Llosa.

While in Montreal, Ross made frequent trips to New York; now, when he can afford it, he visits London, Paris, Rome, Athens, or Barcelona. His cosmopolitan interests—linguistic, artistic, and personal—contradict the generally received notion of Sinclair Ross, simple prairie boy and bank clerk. A much more complex man than that, he is himself inclined to support—and indeed foster—the simple prairie boy image.

Ross's literary interests also are cosmopolitan. When interviewed upon his retirement he said, "I hope now to have time to reread Proust."[6] This ambition involved the reading of the twenty-two volumes of *A la recherche du temps perdu*. He says now, "I've never got around to it and I'm sure I never will." Ross admires, besides the South Americans, Dostoevski, especially *Crime and Punishment* and *The Brothers Karamazov;* Faulkner, for in particular *As I Lay Dying, The Sound and the Fury,* and *Light in August;* Joyce's *Ulysses;* Hardy's *Return of the Native;* Hemingway's *The Sun Also Rises* and *A Farewell to Arms.* Other French writers he has read and admired are Camus, Gide, Malraux, François Mauriac, and Claude Mauriac. An early Canadian novel which made an impact on him was Martha Ostenso's *Wild Geese;* He has not read Frederick Philip Grove. Another novel which impressed him at an early age—about twenty—was Aldous Huxley's *Point Counterpoint*[7]. It is obvious that Sinclair Ross is himself very perceptive, widely read, and very conscious of contemporary literary developments.

Ross's attitude to writing, one to which he continues to hold, as recent conversations with him confirm is expressed in a letter in 1970:

. . . artists themselves as well as psychologists seem pretty well agreed that the "creative sources" are in the subconscious, and the psychologists are also agreed that self-analysis can seldom do more than scrape the surface. . . . So if I don't understand myself—my "creative processes" if you like, why I did this and not that—how could I possibly write about them?[8]

Ross's creative sources, because they do come from the subconscious as he says, are therefore, inexplicable. However, he does have very clear ideas on the role of the artist whom he views as observant and sensitive and one who seeks to share his perceptions with others. Ross's craft is "conscious." He writes many drafts and carefully revises for economy and rhythm. Although a writer of spare, taut prose, he is very conscious of cadence. The economy and simplicity of his language are deceptive as his writing has an unexpected subtlety and depth. His language, often metaphoric, has the compression and intensity of poetry.

Sinclair Ross is a quiet man who has never married and remains basically a loner. Although friendly and sociable, he cherishes his privacy. In Malaga he lives in an apartment overlooking the Mediterranean. Although he enjoys music, reading, trips to Athens, Rome, London, and walks in the country, his main interest continues to be literature.

CHAPTER 2

Short Stories

T HE medium is the message in Ross's remarkable prairie stories. The prairie environment, which is both backdrop and antagonist, is also the medium through which the inner world of his individuals is revealed.

Ross has published eighteen stories. They appeared in a variety of periodicals: *Queen's Quarterly, Nash's Pall-Mall, Manitoba Arts Review, The Country Guide and Nor'west Farmer,* and *Journal of Canadian Fiction.* The majority appeared first in *Queen's Quarterly,* and most were published between 1934 and 1952. Ten are collected in *The Lamp at Noon and Other Stories* (1968).[1]

Each story is a finely wrought pattern of event, character, and setting in which precision, economy, rhythm, and repetition, the hallmarks of Ross's novels, are evident. Most of the stories are set on the prairie and portray the struggles of the prairie farmer and his family during the drought and depression of the nineteen-thirties. While recreating the prairie of the depression, this fiction most often concentrates on the effect of loneliness, isolation, hardship, and poverty on individuals and their relationships. Thus, although Ross vividly and realistically portrays the wind, storms, and droughts of the prairie of the thirties, his focus is on inner rather than outer reality. In fact, one of the remarkable aspects of his art is his ability to merge inner and outer landscape. It is this quality of his writing which has been most frequently commented upon by his critics. Margaret Laurence, in her introduction to *The Lamp at Noon and Other Stories,* points out that "the outer situation always mirrors the inner. The emptiness of the landscape, the bleakness of the land, reflect the inability of these people to touch another with assurance and gentleness."[2] Earlier Roy Daniells comments on the correspondence of inner and outer worlds in Ross's first novel, writing in his introduction to the 1957 edition of *As For Me and My House:* "The inner and outer worlds of the Bentleys correspond perfectly, but there's no need to think of symbolism or of a mirror-image, for the truth is that in the simplest fashion their lives are the product of living in such an environment."[3] John Moss underlines the same point when he says, "There is a fine reciprocity between the internal and the external worlds of Ross's characters—. . . . His prairie stories and novels echo the Blakean dictum that man in a generative world becomes what he beholds."[4] The most thorough exploration of this facet of Ross's writing is that of Laurence Ricou in his study *Vertical Man/Horizontal World: Man and Landscape in Canadian Prairie Fiction*. Ricou directs attention primarily to this aspect of Ross's writing in his chapter on Ross, "The Prairie Internalized." Although Ricou deals primarily with *As For Me and My House*, he is speaking of the totality of Ross's work when he says: "Ross is the first writer in Canada to show a profound awareness of the metaphorical possibilities of the prairie landscape. More particularly, and hence the term 'internalization' is appropriate, Ross introduces the landscape as a metaphor for man's mind, his emotions, his soul perhaps, in a more thorough and subtle way than any previous writer."[5] It is appropriate that Ross, who goes beyond the realism of prairie novelists before him to focus on the psychological impact which environment has on his individuals and their relation with others, uses the setting itself as metaphor for expression of this inner reality. Images from the world they inhabit and to which they react give expression to the individuals themselves and define their actions.

The bleakest of Ross's stories were published between 1934 and 1941, prior to the publication of his first novel. At this time Ross had left the small Saskatchewan towns where he observed at first hand the combination of economic and environmental disasters which wrought havoc on the prairies during the years of the Great Depression. While Ross continued to write of the West, later stories, which include "One's a Heifer," "The Outlaw," and "The Runaway," possess much less of the bleakness and despair of the early stories.

I *Ross's First Story*

Ross's first story, "No Other Way," was published in *Nash's Pall-Mall* in October 1934, after winning third prize in that magazine's short story competition. It demonstrates a number of the stylistic characteristics and thematic preoccupations which Ross was to continue to develop.

The central character of this story is Hatty Glenn, a middle-aged woman who appears older than she is after twenty years struggling against the vicissitudes of farm life: "The thin, hatchety face and the yellow neck; the tight little knot of iron-grey hair; the wrinkles and crowsfeet. That was what the years and the slaving had done."[6] The change in Hatty is not merely physical. In personality as well as appearance she is a different person from the young woman who had married Dan twenty years earlier. For as her husband has grown away from her Hatty has become increasingly nagging, bitter and parsimonious. Dan has been successful in his shrewd maneuvering with wheat and land deals, while Hatty, by dint of sheer hard work, has made a success of the farm itself. Thus while he has retained his youthful, handsome appearance, she has become wrinkled and haggard. Ironically, Hatty has lost her husband through her devotion to a cause she thought they shared, the success of their farm. Events of the story take place at the moment when Hatty realizes that she has lost Dan's love irrevocably.

In "No Other Way" Ross reveals his concern with interpersonal relationships, with love and the loss of love. He presents the interplay between husband and wife against a setting which is a contributing factor in their relationship. In this first story Ross shows his first-hand knowledge of farm life: of vegetables to be stored, fences to be repaired, stoves to be cleaned, and the endless multitude of chores which make up a prairie woman's day. More importantly, he demonstrates what years of exhausting struggle can do to a marriage. The portrait of Hatty Glenn is the first of many portraits by Ross of prairie farm wives, disappointed, old before their time, aware that they are no longer loved. At the moment when Hatty comes face to face with her situation, she contemplates suicide, to then realize that there is "no other way" than to continue, stoically, as she has for twenty years, to struggle alone with the farm work.

Rather than presenting the drought and depression which pervade so many of Ross's stories, "No Other Way" presents the successful farm; but as with his novel *The Well*, written twenty-four years later, the protagonist looks back to the early years of hardship as the happy years. In this story as in the later novel, an old unused well is the focal point for recollections of past happiness:

. . . she came to the bleached cribbing of an old, unused well.
She looked at it reflectively, remembering how her arms used to ache when she had to pull up water with a rope and pail, before they drilled the

new well and could afford a windmill. There was an old roan cow that used to drink eight pailfuls, night and morning, and then leave the trough reluctantly.

And yet, that had been the vital, solid time of her life. The work had a purpose behind it; there had been something to look forward to. It used to seem that a windmill, and a big house with carpets and a gramophone, were all that was needed to make life perfect: and now, after all the old wishes had been realised, here she was, back at the well. (82)

The antimaterialistic theme of the later novel, *The Well,* and the central symbol of the well itself, are first evident in this story. In the novel, the well is more skillfully woven into the texture of the work, as a symbol of vital, purposeful activity and of shared love—and as a link between past and present, between illusion and reality. It is interesting that the antimaterialism which is viewed by most critics of *The Well* as a comment on the affluence of the late 1950's was evident in a story writtten in the early depression years. Other themes developed in "No Other Way" which continue to concern Ross in later works include entrapment, which is well defined by the title of the story,[7] the strength and endurance which characterize Ross's individuals, and the rupture of communication between husband and wife.

Stylistically, also, the story provides an indication of the course Ross is to follow in future works. The first sentence prefigures one of the most outstanding characteristics of Ross's style, his metaphoric use of nature: "Out of a sprawling sunset, ragged and unkempt, as if in a sullen mood it had grown careless of itself, the October wind dragged a clamping, resolute night" (16). In this sentence, the image itself and the symbol are awkward in comparison with Ross's later more subtle use of imagery and smoother, less stilted phrasing, yet it is an appropriate image for this account of a bitter, unkempt, and sullen woman and her attempt to influence her resolutely indifferent husband. Except for one brief revelation of Dan's thoughts, the third-person narrative is told from the point of view of the wife, the narrative point of view which characterizes most of Ross's later stories of prairie farmers and their wives. The momentary shift in viewpoint is unexpected and inappropriate, the technical failing of a less experienced writer. The irony present in most of Ross's writings is evident in the dilemma of Hatty Glenn who realizes that she has lost her husband through her excessive devotion to the farm which she had considered to be their shared concern. The story is cyclic; it begins and ends with Hatty chasing cows out of the turnips, a scene not without humor, but a scene signifying Hatty's entrapment. Her situation remains the same at the end of the story as it was at the beginning.

"No Other Way" lacks the subtlety and psychological complexity which are to be major sources of strength in Ross's writing: the emotional intensity is less, handling of voice not as skillful, and prose style not always as graceful as that of succeeding stories. Nevertheless, it points clearly the direction which Ross is going to take.

II *The Farm Wife*

The sense of isolation and failure of communication, paramount in those stories told from a woman's point of view, are voiced with most intensity in "The Painted Door" and "The Lamp at Noon."

A. The Painted Door

In "The Painted Door" Ann gives vent to her frustration at the loneliness and drabness of her life as a prairie farm wife. Her slow, plodding husband has been made duller and more silent by the exhausting demands of farm labor. Ironically, his devotion to her has pushed him to work even harder to pay off the mortgage, so that he can do even more for her, build her a new house and buy her pretty clothes. The story relates events leading to Ann's seduction by the younger, more handsome neighbor as she waits alone for her husband, John, to return from his father's farm five miles away. When the young neighbor, Steven, arrives to spend the evening Ann sees in him all that John lacks: for Steven is handsome, clean-shaven, erect, assured. No sooner has she capitulated to Steven, persuaded by him that not even John can get home in the blizzard now raging, than she realizes the superficiality of his attractions in contrast with John's substantial qualities. For John may be slow and dull, but he is reliable and devoted. His lack of grace and polish is insignificant in contrast with his enduring loyalty and love. Ann now perceives: "John was the man. With him lay all the future. For tonight, slowly and contritely through the day[s] and years to come, she would try to make amends."[8] But Ann's repentance comes too late and the stunning finale tells the reader as it tells Ann that she must bear for the rest of her life the consequences of her one momentary weakness.

This story exemplifies Ross's use of landscape to mirror inner reality. The coldness, barrenness, and loneliness of the setting are the cause of Ann's situation as well as a reflection of her own inner sense of loneliness and isolation. The storm impending as John leaves her for his father's farm mirrors her own impending emotional storm; and throughout the day, as the storm outside becomes increasingly violent, so too does her own emotional state become increasingly distraught. The words applied to the physical storm outside, "The storm wrenched the walls as if to make them buckle in" (113), apply equally to her own inner state as she struggles against Steven's attractiveness.

Steven, who is cold, insolent, and passionless, is linked with the coldness of the exterior winter climate. In contrast, John's devotion and Ann's attempts to remind herself of his love and withstand her own rebellious feelings are linked with the fire and warmth, and with her endeavors throughout the day to build up the fire. Her attempt to ward off the encroaching cold parallels her attempt to withstand her attraction to Steven. This complex interweaving of inner and outer states is initiated at the beginning of the story with Ann's warning to John of the coming storm and John's words, which in retrospect are proven to be disastrously wrong, "But there's nothing to be afraid of—" (99)? Ann's resentment against John for leaving her alone is apparent in the coldness of her voice as well as by the words of her reply, "It was a curiously cold voice now, as if the words were chilled by their contact with the frosted pane. 'Plenty to eat—plenty of wood to keep me warm—what more could a woman ask for?' " (99) The loneliness, bleakness and bitter cold of the landscape are then viewed through Ann's eyes:

The sun was risen above the frost mists now, so keen and hard a glitter on the snow that instead of warmth its rays seemed shedding cold. One of the two-year-old colts that had cantered away when John turned the horses out for water stood covered with rime at the stable door again, head down and body hunched, each breath a little plume of steam against the frosty air. She shivered, but did not turn. In the clear, bitter light the long white miles of prairie landscape seemed a region alien to life. Even the distant farmsteads she could see served only to intensify a sense of isolation. Scattered across the face of so vast and bleak a wilderness it was difficult to conceive them as a testimony of human hardihood and endurance. Rather they seemed futile, lost, to cower before the implacability of snow-swept earth and clear pale sun-chilled sky. (100)

Simple, spare diction echoes the bleak, remorseless landscape. Description repetitively insists upon its emptiness and loneliness: "long white miles of prairie landscape seemed a region alien to life"; "so vast and bleak a wilderness"; "distant farmsteads . . . intensify a sense of isolation"; "scattered . . . they seemed futile, lost."

As soon as John leaves, Ann becomes aware of the silence and chill: "It was the silence weighing upon her—the frozen silence of the bitter fields and sun-chilled sky—lurking outside as if alive, relentlessly in wait, mile-deep between her now and John" (102). Steven, too, like the cold is "relentlessly in wait," as not only the physical but also the emotional gulf between Ann and John widens. Throughout the day Ann tries to maintain her serenity and her loyalty to John; she busies herself with her painting and builds up the fire against the silence, isolation, and encroaching cold. Ann's discontent, increasingly difficult to stifle as the day passes, continues to be reflected by the description of the cold: "It was getting cold again, and she left her painting to put in more wood. But this time the warmth spread slowly" (105).

When Ann must leave the house to feed the farm animals she is unable to withstand the violence of the blizzard; she struggles back to the house, defeated by the storm and terrified at its intensity: "Only her body pressing hard like this against the door was staving it off. She didn't dare move" (109). Later, when she feels Steven's attraction, Ann herself links him with the storm: "It was less Steven himself that she felt than his inevitability. Just as she had felt the snow, the silence and the storm" (111), and finally, when his attraction overwhelms her as did the storm earlier, she associates her sensations with the feeling she had earlier when attempting to stave off the storm: "It was the same as a few hours ago when she braced the door against the storm. He was watching her, smiling. She dared not move, unclench her hands, or raise her eyes. The flames crackled, the clock ticked. The storm wrenched the walls as if to make them buckle in. So rigid and desperate were all her muscles set, withstanding, that the room around her seemed to swim and reel. So rigid and strained that for relief at last, despite herself, she raised her head and met his eyes again" (113). Again the stark simplicity of diction and phrasing underlines the tension. Except for the one word, "smiling," which describes Steven, there are no modifiers in this passage, no adverbs or adjectives, until the repeated, "So rigid

and desperate. . . . So rigid and strained. . . ," which by the insistent, incantatory rhythm contributes to the depiction of her in-
evitable surrender. This is the moment of her capitulation and now,
no longer struggling against the storm within herself, she feels "as if
the storm had lulled, as if she had suddenly found calm and shelter"
(113 - 14).

The cold and storm outside operate as a synecdoche to represent the harshness of land and climate which after seven years have
caused Ann to rebel against the bleakness and loneliness of her life
and against her plodding, devoted husband. It is appropriate that
John should wander back out into the storm after he has discovered
Ann and Steven together, since the storm is a reflection of Ann's internal storm which caused her to betray him. She was defeated by
cold and loneliness of which the cold, passionless Steven is both
symbol and agent. John, who, because of his dogged loyalty and
devotion, has fought his way through the blizzard to her, freezes to
death, a victim not of the snow and cold but of his wife's betrayal.

Handling of time contributes to the effectiveness of this story.
There are two kinds of time: linear, objective time, the one day in
which events occur; and subjective time, the monotonous,
repetitive seven years of their marriage and all the dreary years yet
to come as Ann imaginatively relives the past and looks into the
future: "But now, alone with herself in the winter silence, she saw
the spring for what it really was. This spring—next spring—all the
springs and summers still to come. While they grew old, while their
bodies warped, while their minds kept shrivelling dry and empty
like their lives" (105). The texture of Ross's prose approximates the
tone and emotional tension of the situation. In this quotation
rhythm and repetition echo the endless monotony Ann sees ahead
of her. The repetition of the word "spring" and the incantatory
rhythm reflect the endless monotonous life Ann sees ahead: "This
spring—next spring—all the springs and summers still to come."
Short, terse phrases underline the sexual tension; as over and over
again the same words "the flames crackled, the clock ticked" intensify the silence and pressure. Subjective time superimposed upon
the present makes this day insupportable for Ann and helps the
reader to understand the loneliness, despair, and need which result
in her surrender to Steven. For Steven, young, well-groomed,
smooth talking—all that John is not—becomes a symbol of all that
is missing in her life. Although Ann's true sense of values soon
reasserts itself and she sees the superficiality of Steven's attractions

in contrast to the genuineness of John's qualities, her realization comes too late. The vastness, loneliness, and harshness of the environment which have made John slower and duller, Ann more morose and dissatisfied, finally defeat them.

B. The Lamp at Noon

"A little before noon she lit the lamp. Demented wind fled keening past the house."[9] In these terse opening sentences of "The Lamp at Noon" the wind goes beyond mirroring the young woman's turmoil to foreshadowing her fate: "There were two winds: the wind in flight, and the wind that pursued. The one sought refuge in the eaves, whimpering in fear; the other assailed it there, and shook the eaves apart to make it flee again" (14). The sand sifts into the house and the wind shrieks into the eaves, penetrating Ellen's mind as they invade her house.

In "The Lamp at Noon" as in "The Painted Door" the harshness of the struggle with the land overwhelms the young wife. For five years Paul and Ellen have been dried out; now a three-day sandstorm leaves the land once more a desert. Paul, grimly enduring the years of drought and dust and continuing to hope the land will come back, is unaware of the extent of his wife's desperation. The growing rift between them is evidenced by their bitter quarrelling. Ellen feels caged, trapped by wind, dust and her own inability to act. Like Ann in "The Painted Door," who realized too late that "John was the man," Paul understands his wife's viewpoint too late. By then she has fled into the storm with her baby. When he finds them she is mad and the child has suffocated.

The author repeats the words "see" and "blind" to indicate the opposition of the two protagonists: Paul clings to his dream and is blind to his wife's lonely terror and her need of him; Ellen has no dream of the future but sees all too clearly the wasted years of the past and of the future. Ross underlines Ellen's inability to shut out reality—past, present or future—by frequent mention of her inability to shut her eyes. As she looks out at the storm, "Her eyes all the while were fixed and wide with a curious immobility. . . . Now she could not close them." As T. S. Eliot says in "Burnt Norton," "human kind / Cannot bear very much reality."[10] Ellen has reached her breaking point. The tragedy is that her husband does not realize her desperation. Fear of emotion and inability to express tenderness, prominent problems of Ross's farmers and their wives, are all too evident in this relationship. Ellen anxiously watches for Paul's return to the house, wanting his nearness but knowing "he would only despise her if she ran to the stable looking for him" (14). When she hears his approach she busies herself about the stove, although she wants "to feel his arms supporting her, to cry a little just that he might soothe her" (15). When she does, finally, ask him to stay with her that afternoon, he refuses, and when he later returns, worried, to peer in the window at her he is "careful, despite his concern, not to reveal a fear or weakness that she might think capitulation to her wishes" (20 - 21). Such determined barricading of oneself from another, such refusal to demonstrate care or tenderness, is the consequence of years of stubbornly withstanding the harshness and bleakness of nature. The failure of communication extends to a failure on Paul's part not only to see what is happening to his wife now but to see what is happening to their farm, to himself, and to his relationship with his wife.

Ross insistently applies the word "blind" to Paul. First, through his wife, Ellen, who argues "Look at the sky—what's happening. Are you blind? Thistles and tumbleweeds—it's a desert. You won't have a straw this fall" (16). Ellen then directly accuses Paul of blindness; she pleads with him: "Look at it—look at it, you fool. Desert—the lamp lit at noon—" (16). But Paul is blind also to her situation, trapped in a life of unending poverty, and to her desperation, although "The spent quietness in her voice was even harder to endure than her anger. It reproached him, against his will insisted that he see and understand her lot" (17). Ellen tries desperately to make him see what has happened to the land: "Will you never see? It's the land itself—the soil. You've plowed and harrowed it until there's not a root or fibre left to hold it down. That's why the soil drifts—that's why in a year or two there'll be nothing left but the bare clay" (17). Paul's only response is to sit "staring at the lamp." While a lamp is a symbol of hope, at the same time to light the lamp at noon is a symbol of the darkness of their situation.

Paul will not look at his wife or at what is happening to her; he will not look at the land and what is happening to it. He is happier when he can escape from Ellen into the "vast darkness" of the stable where he will not be asked to see. But alone in the stable he considers Ellen's words: "But all the time was he only a blind and stubborn fool? Was Ellen right? Was he trampling on her life, and throwing away his own? The five years since he married her, were they to go on repeating themselves, five, ten, twenty, until all the brave future he looked forward to was but a stark and futile past?" (20). At this moment finally, he sees: "She looked forward to no future. She had no faith or dream with which to make the dust and poverty less real. He understood suddenly. He saw her face again as only a few minutes ago it had begged him not to leave her" (20). Yet he still does not return to comfort her for fear of appearing weak. Hearing Ellen scream in the sound of the wind, picturing her eyes pleading, imagining her running headlong into the storm, Paul remains working in the barn. This demonstration of machismo is typical of the majority of Ross's males, who do not dare show emotion or tenderness.

When the wind dies and Paul can once more see the fields which the sandstorm had obliterated, he has a second moment of vision. The sight of the devastated fields leads to a deeper vision:

Suddenly the fields before him struck his eyes to comprehension. They lay black, naked. Beaten and mounded smooth with dust as if a sea in gentle swell had turned to stone. And though he had tried to prepare himself for such a scene, though he had known since yesterday that not a blade would last the storm, still now, before the utter waste confronting him, he sickened and stood cold. Suddenly like the fields he was naked. Everything that had sheathed him a little from the realities of existence: vision and purpose, faith in the land, in the future, in himself—it was all rent now, stripped away. "Desert," he heard her voice begin to sob. "Desert, you fool—the lamp lit at noon!" (21 - 22)

No longer sheathed from "the realities of existence," as if a blindfold had been lifted, Paul finally can see. He understands Ellen's fear and terror, sees the rightness of her advice about fibrous crops, sees that the land has become a desert, sees that his own faith in the future had been an illusion. But his revelation has come too late. Ross describes with stark brevity the scene that greets Paul when he finally returns to the house. "The door was open, the lamp blown out, the crib empty" (22). The extinguished lamp symbolizes the extinction of Ellen's hope, her capitulation to despair; the open door indicates nature's invasion of man's garrison, nature's victory over man; the empty crib foreshadows the death of the child and of Paul's dream of establishing a family on this land. The final, bitter irony is expressed in the last line, in words spoken by Ellen: " 'So still now, and a red sky—it means tomorrow will be fine' " (23). Their tomorrow will not be fine. In an ironic reversal, now Paul sees the real world, but Ellen, who viewed reality too clearly to be sustainable, has passed into an illusory world.

III *Childhood*

A. A Day with Pegasus

"A Day with Pegasus" explores the theme of childhood fantasy
versus adult reality, a theme explored also in "Circus in Town" and
"The Outlaw." In all three stories a horse plays a central role in the
child's fantasy life.

"A Day with Pegasus" takes the reader into the mind of nine-
year-old Peter Parker on the day his long awaited colt is born. As
Peter excitedly considers names for his colt those that come to his
mind are such regal ones as King and Prince; whereas his mother
suggests, "Bill's a good name. . . . Short and sensible. Or Mike, or
Joe. We had a Buster once—before your time." [11] Thus are stolid,
earthbound adults contrasted with marvelling children.

Unable and unwilling to break out of the dream into which the
colt has propelled him, Peter finds adults equally unable to comprehend his imaginative world. The portrait of Peter's teacher, Miss
Kinley, is particularly unsympathetic. When Peter writes a composition on how he spent last Saturday, she is aghast at his description
of a rodeo and a colorfully dressed cowboy named Slim:

"How could you, Peter? Stand up and answer me. How could you?
Rodeos—*cowboys*—you surely didn't expect me to believe—"
She was more distressed than angry. It was something she had never en-
countered before, something that evaded her ordinary, time-tried
classifications of good conduct and bad. "You haven't a horse at all. You
were at home on Saturday. I drove past your place on my way to town, and
you were in the garden with your brother planting potatoes."
"Yes," he nodded quickly, "that was it—Saturday I planted potatoes all
day."
"Then why didn't you obey me? Why did you write all this?"
He glanced up and met her eyes, wondering hopelessly how to make her
understand. "Because it wasn't worth writing about—because it was just
planting potatoes."
"And you think that's excuse enough for all these lies?"
"But they aren't lies, Miss Kinley—not real lies."
She pursed her lips. "You mean you do have a horse—and it did run a
race and win a hundred dollars?"
"No—not really—not yet—."
Again she pursed her lips, then turned quickly and spoke over her
shoulder. "That's all then, for now. You'd better go outside and play for a
few minutes. I'll have to keep you after school to write another composition." (115 - 16)

Despite a detention with the uncomprehending Miss Kinley and a fight with an equally uncomprehending schoolmate who referred to the colt as a "nag," Peter is undaunted. As soon as he sees the colt again he is back in the world of fantasy, the world of Pegasus:

There was a state of mind, a mood, a restfulness, in which one could skim along this curve of prairie floor and, gathering momentum from the downward swing, glide up again and soar away from earth. He succeeded now, borne by a white-limbed steed again. And as they soared the mystery was not solved, but gradually absorbed, a mystery still but intimate, a heartening gleam upon the roof of life to let him see its vault and spaciousness. (118)

The story reveals not only the excitement and wonder of the child but the overly literal, harsh, and unimaginative attitude of the adult unable to comprehend a child's fantasies. The third-person narrative is recounted entirely from Peter's point of view. His thoughts, dreams, actions and reactions make up the story. Although focusing on this one momentous day in the boy's life, the author also reveals the daily round of farm chores, school and family life. The colt provides an agent of escape from the dreary and restricted routine of Peter's limited world, for it carries him into a world of unknown possibilities which adults are shown to have long forgotten. This is one of Ross's most optimistic stories. Peter remains undaunted by the repressive attitude of adults. Although the young boy would not recognize the name Pegasus or its significance, the story is appropriately named. Pegasus, the winged horse, carries Peter into an exciting new world.

B. Circus in Town

"Circus in Town" also explores a young child's imaginative life, this time against the backdrop of adult bickering and dissatisfaction. Eleven-year-old Jenny's brother brings her a torn piece of poster which he has found on the street of the nearby town. "A girl in purple tights, erect on a galloping horse, a red-coated brass band, a clown, an elephant ripped through the middle."[12] For Jenny, the poster represents a novel, exciting world: "The bit of poster had spun a new world before her, excited her, given wild, soaring impetus to her imagination; and now, without in the least understanding herself, she wanted the excitement and the soaring, even though it might stab and rack her, rather than the barren satisfaction of believing that in life there was nothing better, nothing more vivid or dramatic, than her own stableyard" (68).

Jenny is too young to realize that to her parents the torn poster represents something quite different. To her mother it represents all the things she wants for her daughter but realizes she will never have: "Look at her clothes and her bare feet! Your own daughter! Why don't you take hold—do something? Nothing ahead of her but chickens and cows!" (69). To her father it is a reproach, a symbol of his inability to provide even the simplest of pleasures for his family. Her parents' bitter quarrelling, instigated by the poster, dismays the child but does not dampen her imagination and excitement. "All night long she wore her purple tights and went riding Billie round and round the pasture in them. A young, fleet-footed Billie. Caparisoned in blue and gold and scarlet, silver bells on reins and bridle-neck arched proudly to the music of the band" (72).

Ross has chosen a simple incident to delineate and contrast the hopeful imagination of children for whom the future still holds promise of excitement and glamor, with the disillusion and frustration of adults painfully aware how little they can offer their children beyond the harsh, drab lives they know themselves.

C.   Cornet at Night

In several stories where the first-person narrator is a young boy, a retrospective narrative is told. This produces the dual focus of the child's viewpoint of events at the same time commented upon from the adult perspective. In "Cornet at Night" the narrative voice is that of Tommy, now grown up and remembering events which occurred when he was eleven years old. The story is written in such a way that the narrative voice speaks for the two points of view simultaneously: the reader is made to comprehend the child's sensibility, to experience his thoughts and emotions; at the same time the retrospective voice provides a framework for the interpretation of these events and for achieving insight into the other characters as well. From time to time an illuminating comment is made from the adult perspective, such as the following: "For a farm boy is like that. Alone with himself and his horse he cuts a fine figure. He is the measure of the universe. He foresees a great many encounters with life, and in them all acquits himself a little more than creditably. He is fearless, resourceful, a bit of a brag. His horse never contradicts."[13] The double focus affects the tone of the story, which is more objective and at times more wryly ironic than it would be if a young boy embroiled in the situation were reporting it directly. Thus the adult looking back can describe the runaway, for example, more humorously than could the eleven-year-old youngster:

> . . . and then away went Rock. I'd never have believed he had it in him. With a snort and plunge he was off the road and into the ditch—then out of the ditch again and off at a breakneck gallop across the prairie. There were stones and badger holes, and he spared us none of them. The egg-crates full of groceries bounced out, then the tobacco, then my mother's face powder. "Whoa, Rock!" I cried, "Whoa, Rock!" but in the rattle and whir of wheels I don't suppose he even heard. Philip couldn't help much because he had his cornet to hang on to. I tried to tug on the reins, but at such a rate across the prairie it took me all my time to keep from following the groceries. (46)

As the narrator continues his description of the runaway he shows that he is still in touch with the boyhood perspective: "He was a big horse, Rock, and once under way had to run himself out. Or he may have thought that if he gave us a thorough shaking-up we would be too subdued when it was over to feel like taking him seriously to task" (46). Here the first remark gives a generally accepted adult explanation, whereas the second reveals the voice of the boy to whom the horse is a companion, thinking and reacting much as he would himself.

In this story eleven-year-old Tommy makes his first trip to town alone, as his father is too busy with the harvest to go himself. Tommy has received complicated instructions for selling eggs and buying groceries:

> . . . both quantity and quality of some of the groceries were to be determined by the price of eggs. Thirty cents a dozen, for instance, and I was to ask for coffee at sixty-five cents a pound. Twenty-nine cents a dozen and coffee at fifty cents a pound. Twenty-eight and no oranges. Thirty-one and bigger oranges. It was like decimals with Miss Wiggins, or two notes in the treble against three in the bass. For my father a tin of special blend tobacco, and my mother not to know. For my mother a box of face powder at the drugstore, and my father not to know. Twenty-five cents from my father on the side for ice-cream and licorice. Thirty-five from my mother for my dinner at the Chinese restaurant. And warnings, of course, to take good care of Rock, speak politely to Mr. Jenkins, and see that I didn't get machine oil on my corduroys. (39)

Tommy's most important mission is to find a farm hand to assist with the harvest. At the restaurant he meets a young man different from any he has met before: "Different from the farmer boys I knew, yet different also from the young man with the yellow shoes in Jenkins' store. Staring out at it through the restaurant window he was as far away from Main Street as was I with plodding old Rock and my squeaky corduroys" (42). Against his better judgment the boy brings this stranger, Philip Coleman, a cornet player, home with him. Although Phil proves to be a failure at stooking hay and is packed off the next day, his music brings a moment of beauty into the lives of Tommy and his parents. For a few minutes they are transported into a different world and forget the pressures of everyday existence. The boy's parents, although they are moved by the playing, are nevertheless compelled to be realistic:

Then my mother called, and I had to slip away fast so that she would think I was coming from the bunkhouse. "I hope he stooks as well as he plays," she said when I went in. "Just the same, you should have done as your father told you, and picked a likelier man to see us through the fall."

My father came in from the stable then, and he, too, had been listening. With a wondering, half-incredulous little movement of his head he made acknowledgment. (50)

A major theme of the story is summed up in the final stark statement, "A harvest, however lean, is certain every year; but a cornet at night is golden only once" (51). Ross develops this theme more fully in *Whir of Gold* in which the elusive beauty of music and a young man's attempt to capture it provide the central focus. As gold in this story is associated with the cornet and with music, gold in *Whir of Gold* is again the central symbol.

Beneath the surface several other themes are interwoven. An undercurrent of discontent is evident in the disagreement between Tommy's parents about working on Sunday, taking the boy out of school to go to town, giving him music lessons. As in "Circus in Town" the child becomes the focal point for the parents' quarrelling, especially for the mother's dissatisfaction. Her pent-up resentment flares out in response to her husband's "When I was his age I didn't even get to school," and she replies, "Exactly, . . . and look at you today. Is it any wonder I want him to be different?" (36). With gentle humor Ross describes the mother's attempts to observe the proprieties of Sunday. Unable to attend church because her husband is too busy with the harvest, she and the boy spend their day in the parlor dressed in their Sunday clothes, reading the Bible and playing hymns, "for, fearing visitors, my mother was resolved to let them see that she and I were uncontaminated by my father's sacrilege" (37). Young Philip Coleman's story is only hinted at in his explanation of his presence in the prairie town: "They tell me a little toughening up is what I need. Outdoors, and plenty of good hard work—so I'll be like the fellow that just went out" [a tough, unshaven farm hand] (44). Failing abysmally as a farm hand he returns to town carrying a box of lunch and ointment for his sunburn.

In revising this story for publication in *A Lamp at Noon and Other Stories,* Ross made more changes (mostly excisions) in this than in other republished stories. A minor, yet appropriate, change is that of the horse's name from Jupiter to Rock, a name indicative of his usual stolid, plodding nature. The major changes occur in two incidents concerning the young musician and the boy's response to him. In the first instance Tommy recalls his emotions when he heard Philip play:

And I remember still what a long and fearful moment it was, waiting for him to begin. I crouched still, unbreathing, steeled for the beauty that I knew must come. Steeled because I knew it would be piercing beauty—beauty that must cleave and widen life for room to shape itself, to cast its span.

At last he began; and the notes that came did pierce, and they did give life expanse that it had never had before. Like the cornet itself they were eloquent and golden. They floated up against the night, and each for a moment hung there clear and visible. Sometimes they mounted poignant and sheer. Sometimes they soared, and then curved tenderly towards earth again. And always their beauty was a lonely beauty. Only for Philip there I could not have endured it. With my senses I clung to the smell of his tobacco smoke, to the pale faint whiteness of his fingers on the cornet keys. I was afraid of losing him, afraid of having to confront alone the abysmal beauty that his music had revealed. And yet all the time I knew I must. This way of brief lost gleam against the night was my way too. And alone I cowered a moment, understanding that there could be no escape, no other way. [14]

These paragraphs have been shortened and tightened to convey the same sensations but more tautly and economically:

And I remember still what a long and fearful moment it was, crouched and steeling myself, waiting for him to begin.

And I was right: when they came the notes were piercing, golden as the cornet itself, and they gave life expanse that it had never known before. They floated up against the night, and each for a moment hung there clear and visible. Sometimes they mounted poignant and sheer. Sometimes they soared and then, like a bird alighting, fell and brushed earth again." (49)

In the much shorter revised passage Ross has deleted vague, repetitious remarks, such as, "I knew it would be piercing beauty—beauty that must cleave and widen life for room to shape itself, to cast its span" and, "Like the cornet itself they [the notes] were eloquent and golden"; and has eliminated those passages in which the boy speaks of his realization that "this way of the brief lost gleam against the night" is his way too. He has added the simile "then like a bird alighting. . . ."

Later, in the scene in which Philip is about to leave, a second specific reference to Tommy's future is eliminated. The first version, with future cuts bracketed, reads: "[Fiercely] I wanted to rebel against what was happening, against the clumsiness and crudity of life, but instead I stood quiet, almost passive, [controlled by a resignation that seemed ultimate. For I knew that this was the beginning—the first step along the way that already I had acknowledged as my own. Gravely I shook hands with him, and] then, wheeling away,[15] carried out his cornet to the buggy."[16] In both these examples of revisions Ross eliminated the lines which specifically indicate that Tommy now sees he too must be a musician—or at least an artist. In the revised version Ross leaves the story openended; the focus is on the impact the sheer beauty of the music has on the boy.

Inasmuch as Tommy is brought to the threshold of maturity and understanding, "Cornet at Night" may be considered an initiation story.[17] Tommy achieves new knowledge about the world outside the farm, about men who are different from either the farm boys or the small town men he has known, and about the beauty of music that is different from what he has been taught by Miss Wiggins and her metronome, music that "gave life expanse that it had never known before." He has received some tentative selfknowledge, some awareness of the significance music will have in his own life, an awareness Ross makes more tentative and less fully understood by the boy himself in the revised story.

IV *Initiation Stories*

"The Outlaw" and "One's a Heifer," both stories of thirteen-year-old boys, focus more directly on the initiation theme. According to Mircea Eliade:

The puberty initiation represents above all the revelation of the sacred—and, for the primitive world, the sacred means not only everything that we now understand by religion, but also the whole body of the tribe's mythological and cultural traditions. In a great many cases puberty rites, in one way or another, imply the revelation of sexuality—but, for the entire premodern world, sexuality, too, participates in the sacred. In short, through initiation, the candidate passes beyond the natural mode—the mode of the child—and gains access to the cultural mode; that is, he is introduced to spiritual values.[18]

A. The Outlaw

"The Outlaw," like "A Day with Pegasus," is the story of a boy and his horse. However, the concerns here are very different; an adolescent is tested by an act which has symbolic implications and which includes rebellion against the strictures of childhood. The test involves physical endurance and suffering through which the boy earns acceptance by the adult male in the person of his father, and also wins the admiration of the female in the person of his young schoolmate.

The test involves the beautiful but untamed horse, Isabel. Peter has been forbidden to ride Isabel because of her reputation for throwing anyone who tries. Of course he longs to do so. Isabel is the archetypal horse: "She was one horse, and she was all horses. Thundering battle chargers, fleet Arabians, untamed mustangs—sitting beside her on her manger I knew and rode them all. There was history in her shapely head and burning eyes. I charged with her at Balaklava, Waterloo, scoured the deserts of Africa and the steppes of the Ukraine. Conquest and carnage, trumpets and glory—she understood, and carried me triumphantly."[19] At the same time she is the archetypal female, described variously as "priestess," "temptress," and "queen," with a "perverse, purely feminine itch to bend me to her will" (26).

Isabel did her utmost to convince me that the record was a slander. With muzzling, velvet lips she coaxed and pleaded, whispered that the delights of fantasy and dream were but as shadows beside the exhilarations of reality. Only try reality—slip her bridle on. Only be reasonable—ask myself what she would gain by throwing me. After all, I was turned thirteen. It wasn't as if I were a *small* boy.

And then, temptress, she bore me off to the mountain top of my vanity, and with all the world spread out before my gaze, talked guilefully of prestige and acclaim. (25 - 26)

With these words Ross associates the adolescent and his temptress with the archetypal temptation scene, the temptation of Christ by Satan, as recounted in the Bible: "Again, the devil taketh him up into an exceeding high mountain, and showing him all the kingdoms of the world, and the glory of them: And saith unto him, All these things will I give thee, if thou wilt fall down and worship me."[20] The biblical allusion is not inappropriate. Isabel is clearly associated with temptation and the boy is clearly aware that to ride the horse is to disobey his parents' injunction. Discovery of evil is often a facet of initiation: "An initiation" as Leslie Fiedler says, "is a fall through knowledge to maturity; behind it there persists the myth of the Garden of Eden, the assumption that to know good and evil is to be done with the joy of innocence and to take on the burdens of work and childbearing and death."[21]

Young Millie Dickson, the boy's schoolmate, is the catalyst. It is to impress her that Peter finally does ride Isabel as he has been longing to do. Millie, like Isabel, is a temptress, and the combination of the two Eves is more than a young boy can withstand:

Millie sighed. "I'd like so much though to *see* you ride her. Today—isn't it a good chance, with them in there talking and your father away to town?"

I hesitated, overcome by a feeling of fright and commitment, and then Isabel too joined in. She begged and wheedled, looked so innocent, at the same time so hurt and disappointed, that Millie exclaimed she felt like going for a ride herself. And that settled it. "Stand at the door and see no one's coming," I commanded. "I'll put her bridle on." (29)

As with all initiation rites, this one involves suffering. Not only is the boy thrown by the horse but his ears are severely frozen. It is not too much to suggest that his refusal to listen is appropriately punished by his painfully throbbing ears. Suffering in initiation signifies death to childhood, to asexuality, and to ignorance.[22] The boy's acceptance into the adult male world is indicated by his father's attitude to his venture, which is contrary to that which his mother, still viewing him as a child, has anticipated:

"But the mare," my father interrupted in a man-to-man tone of voice, abruptly cold-shouldering my mother, "how did you find her? Mean as she's supposed to be?"

"Not mean at all. Even when I was getting on—she stood and let me."

"Next time, just the same, you'd better play safe and use a snaffle. I'll hunt one up for you. It won't hurt her so long as she behaves."

"The next time!" my mother cried. "Talking about the next time when you ought to be taking down his breeches. She's no fit horse for a boy. If nobody'll buy her you ought to give her away, before she breaks somebody else's neck."

She went on a long time like that, but I didn't pay much attention. Pride—that was what it amounted to—pride even greater than mine had been before I landed in the snowdrift. It sent me soaring a minute, took my breath away, . . . (33)

The mother's reaction and the boy's "I didn't pay much attention," affirm his rupture with the world of the child, the world associated with the mother. His altered relationship to women includes an altered relationship with Millie, whom the final lines of the story suggest he has won through his heroic actions: "Isabel and the future were all mine. Isabel *and* Millie Dickson" (34). The incident itself symbolizes sexual initiation, with the young mare Peter rides clearly presented as a feminine archetype and a seductress.

The story also demonstrates the transformation of dream into reality. Peter finds that one of his dreams, that of riding Isabel, comes true. How many more of his dreams will he now be able to transform into actuality as he moves from the fantasy world of the child to the real world of the adult: "Outwardly impassive, I was sky-high within. Just as Isabel herself had always said, what a sensation to ride foaming up to school at a breakneck, hair-raising gallop. In the past I had indulged the prospect sparingly. Indeed, with so many threats and warnings in my ears, it had never been a prospect at all, but only a fantasy, something to be thought about wishfully, like blacking both Johnny Olsen's eyes at once, or having five dollars to spend. Now, though, everything was going to be different" (34). His words indicate that, as a result of his initiatory experience, he will now view the world differently.

One specific aspect of this new awareness is his perception of the beauty of the natural world. There is a moment in the adventurous ride when the hero is transformed into the artist and he views the prairie with the eye of the painter:

The prairie spread before us cold and sparkling in the winter sunlight, and poised and motionless, ears pricked forwards, nostrils faintly quivering, she breathed in rapturously its loping miles of freedom.

And I too, responsive to her bidding, was aware as never before of its austere, unrelenting beauty. There were the white fields and the blue, metallic sky; the little splashes here and there of yellow strawstack, luminous and clear as drops of gum on fresh pine lumber; the scattered farmsteads brave and wistful in their isolation; the gleam of sun and snow. I wanted none of it, but she insisted. Thirteen years old and riding an outlaw—naturally I wanted only that. I wanted to indulge shamelessly my vanity, to drink the daring and success of my exploit in full-length draughts, but Isabel, like a conscientious teacher at a fair, dragging you off to see instructive things, insisted on the landscape. (30)

The motif of the artist, central to two of Ross's novels, As For Me and My House and Whir of Gold, is present in a number of stories, most often through the medium of the child, through the child's love of beauty perceived in music as in "Cornet at Night," or the mother's effort to bring some opportunity to her child for a musical or artistic experience remote from the bleakness of his everyday life. In "The Outlaw" it is fitting that Isabel, who is the center of the boy's imaginative life, should be the agent through which he perceives the beauty of the world about him.

Structurally, "The Outlaw" differs from most of Ross's stories. Generally Ross begins quickly: one or two brief introductory sentences lead into an ongoing conversation through which the reader finds himself in the midst of the developing situation. In "The Outlaw," however, fully one-third of the story carefully sets the stage by way of an introduction to Isabel, to the boy's attitude to her and his parents' prohibitions. The remaining two-thirds of the story is divided into two sections; the first is structured around the ride itself and the second focuses on the aftereffects. Young Peter is to appear later as the central figure, Sonny Alpine, in Whir of Gold, where the specific incident of this first ride on Isabel is described in almost the same words in a series of flashbacks to Sonny's Saskatchewan boyhood.

B. One's a Heifer

"One's a Heifer" is narrated from the point of view of the thirteen-year-old farm boy. As with many Ross stories setting initiates action, as the boy sets out in search of two calves lost in a blizzard. Nature is personified and the boy appears as an intruder on the unreceptive landscape: "The deadly cold and the flat white silent miles of prairie asserted themselves like a disapproving presence. The cattle round the straw-stacks stared when we rode up as if we were intruders. The fields stared, and the sky stared. People shivered in their doorways, and said they'd seen no strays."[23]

The story develops into one of mystery and suspense to which the description of setting contributes. The atmosphere becomes increasingly unwelcome as the boy progresses further from home: "But home now seemed a long way off. A thin white sheet of cloud spread across the sky, and though there had been no warmth in the sun the fields looked colder and bleaker without the glitter on the snow. Straw-stacks were fewer here, as if the land were poor, and every house we stopped at seemed more dilapidated than the one before" (120). This is indeed a wasteland. The bleakness reaches its climax with the depiction of the dilapidated farm where the boy caught sight of the calves disappearing: ". . . it was a poor, shiftless-looking place. The yard was littered with old wagons and machinery; the house was scarcely distinguishable from the stables. Darkness was beginning to close in, but there was no light in the windows" (121).

The sense of uneasiness and surprise initiated with the boy's earlier feeling of being an intruder on the prairie increases with the description of the farmer, Vickers, with his wavering look, furtive air, and eccentric behavior. The boy is convinced that, despite Vickers' denials, the calves are in the locked box-stall of his stable. He determines to stay the night and try to get them out while Vickers is sleeping. The boy spends a terrifying night in which he dreams of attempting to get into the stall and at one point wakens to see Vickers acting out a sinister pantomine with an unseen enemy. Finally, just before leaving the next morning, he makes a desperate attempt to break into the locked stall. Vickers attacks him before he can succeed and after a brief struggle the boy escapes from the stable and rides home. It is only with the final lines of the story that the mystery of Vickers' strange and terrifying behavior becomes resolved in the mind of the boy, and of the reader who has been sharing his adventures. With the resolution the full meaning of the story's ironic title becomes apparent. Only at this moment does the boy realize that the calves were not in Vickers' stable; and the impact of what must then have been hidden in the locked stall strikes boy and reader simultaneously: " 'But the stall, then—just because I wanted to look inside he knocked me down—and if it wasn't the calves in there—' She didn't answer. She was busy building up the fire and looking at the stew" (134). The story ends with this contrast between the warm, affectionate world represented by the boy's aunt "building up the fire and looking at the stew" and the nightmare world of the strange, isolated Vickers.

In this as in all the stories of young boys except "A Day with Pegasus," Ross uses the first person point of view. But in method of narration this story differs from others such as "The Outlaw" and "Cornet at Night" in two distinct ways. First, it has a divided protagonist: the young boy is both protagonist and observer; Vickers is an actor in his own story, told partly by the boy and partly through his conversation. The boy, as the first-person narrator, is both inwardly directed, recounting his own adventures, emotions, and impressions in search of the yearlings—and outwardly directed, recounting Vickers' eccentric behavior and his tale of the young woman who had been his housekeeper. A further difference between the narrative method of this and Ross's other stories of farm boys is that, although the story is retrospective, the double focus is not here so apparent; intrusive comments by the adult looking back, such as "I . . . rode erect, as jaunty as the sheepskin and two suits of underwear would permit" (119), are rare. The narrator sustains the viewpoint of the thirteen-year-old more consistently. The youthfulness of the boy opens up an ironic gap between the narrator and the reader, particularly evident in his conversation with Vickers. Here the mature reader can understand the implications of the situation better than the boy. However, the point at which the boy proves to be most unreliable is one which the average reader will miss; that is, the point at which he says that he sees his two yearlings go into Vickers' stable. To reread this incident is to see that Ross has given a clue to the actual situation. The boy says "And then at last I really saw them" (121), referring to the moment when he sees in the distance two yearlings on their way with Vickers' herd into the stable. In the preceding sentence the boy, describing his search, has said, "There were so many cattle straggling across the fields, so many yearlings just like ours. I saw them for sure a dozen times, and as often choked my disappointment down and clicked Tim on again" (121). Since he was mistaken "a dozen times" he could be wrong again this time and Vickers right when Vickers denies that the boy's calves are there. But the reader accepts the narrator's viewpoint so completely by this time that he, with the boy, is convinced that Vickers is lying. And so, until the end of the adventure, the reader assumes with the boy that the calves are in the locked box-stall in Vickers' barn; along with the boy the reader also believes he knows the reason for Vickers' eccentric behavior. Only with the final lines of the story is the truth simultaneously revealed to the boy and to the reader who has been sharing the experiences, that the box-stall contains the body of Vickers' murdered housekeeper.

The initiation rite in "One's a Heifer" involves the thirteen-year-old in a quest which proves to be more difficult and perilous than anticipated. He leaves his aunt, the mother-figure, and, like the mythical hero, leaves his familiar landscape behind to enter strange territory which increasingly takes on the form of a wasteland. The boy undergoes a symbolic descent into hell conveyed by the description of Vickers' farm at which he arrives as darkness closes in and even more clearly conveyed by the menacing dark barn which he enters three times: on his arrival, in his dream, and just before he leaves. The last time he enters the barn he is attacked by Vickers and knocked to the ground; but he recovers to escape back to his own world. Thus the young boy who confronts but is not overcome by evil in the person of Vickers, also symbolically experiences death and rebirth when knocked to the ground. The death-rebirth analogy is reflected also in the night he spends in Vickers' hut. This experience parallels a common initiation rite in which the adolescent is isolated in a dark cabin, symbol of both womb and tomb. The cabin and darkness according to Eliade express "the external psychodrama of a violent death followed by rebirth" (36). The boy's attempt to keep awake during the night so that he might search the barn while Vickers sleeps also parallels an initiation experience. Eliade tells us that "Not to sleep is not only to conquer physical fatigue, but is above all to show proof of will and spiritual strength; to remain awake is to be conscious, present in the world, responsible" (15). The boy's ordeals are both physical and spiritual. Besides physical exhaustion, then, and the attack by Vickers, he must fight off sleep and overcome his own fear. It is significant that as he enters Vickers' cabin, itself a form of underworld, and the tests which will bring him to manhood are about to begin, Vickers greets him as an adult: "Then, as if I were a grown-up, he put out his hand and said, "My name is Arthur Vickers' " (124).

The boy's quest, originally a search for his calves, becomes a search for knowledge, for the revelation of a mystery. Through his dream, a journey into the unconscious, he comes to see that "it wasn't the calves I was looking for after all, and that I still had to see inside the stall" (130). Again, in his last desperate attempt to break into the stall, he realizes that he is "Terrified of the stall, yet compelled by a frantic need to get inside" (132). Despite his seeming failure the boy's quest is successful in a way that in earlier times might be considered magical. First, the calves return home themselves. Also, their return is the final clue to the mystery of the box-stall. The two quests are resolved together, and the two story lines, that of the boy's search and that of Vickers' puzzling behavior, come together at the end. As an initiant, the boy becomes privy to secret knowledge which even the adults of his world do not know. His aunt's reaction to his distraught state, kindly and indulgent but obviously without understanding of what is violently distressing him, further suggests the separation of the boy from the mother-figure and his entrance into the adult world.

V   Nature as Impassive Agent

In many of the early prairie stories the indifference of nature to man is cruelly underlined. Often, indifferent nature is a reflection of, or one aspect of, a cosmic indifference to man's fate. Man is poised on the edge of a void. To Ellen looking out at the dust storm in "The Lamp at Noon," the farmyard seems "an isolated acre, poised aloft above a sombre void. At each blast of wind it shook, as if to topple and spin hurtling with the dust-reel into space" (13). Will in "September Snow," facing the blizzard to rescue his cattle, experiences the same sensation as Ellen: "The snow beneath and around him made it seem he was riding on the top of a cloud. For a while he had the sensation that at every step Bess was about to drop headlong into space."[24]

Man's helplessness in the face of nature is forcefully brought home to Ann in "The Painted Door" where she comes face to face with the immense power of nature: "For a moment her impulse was to face the wind and strike back blow for blow; then, as suddenly as it had come, her frantic strength gave way to limpness and exhaustion. Suddenly, a comprehension so clear and terrifying that it struck all thoughts of the stable from her mind, she realized in such a storm her puniness" (108). The struggle against nature is often bitterly ironic. In "September Snow," Will's young wife dies when left alone while he goes off in the blizzard to search for his cattle. Though he fails in his attempt to bring the cattle back to the shelter of the barn, the next day they return home alone. His fruitless and unnecessary trip contributes to the death of his wife. John, in "The Painted Door," urged on by his devotion to his wife, successfully fights his way home against the storm, a feat no one would consider possible, but returns to find her in the arms of another man.

Chance and coincidence also play their part in deciding man's fate. In "Jug and Bottle," a despairing young soldier commits suicide when he incorrectly assumes that his only friend has turned his back on him. He and his friend mistakenly arrive at different pubs for their rendezvous, and the seeming rejection pushes him into the "void", just as the third day of the dust storm culminating five years of drought has pushed Ellen of "The Lamp at Noon" into madness. Sometimes nature or coincidence works hand in hand with divine retribution. In "The Lamp at Noon," Paul's failure to return to the house to console his wife when he has finally comprehended her feelings, leads to a dead child and an insane wife. In "The Runaway" Luke Taylor's own meanness and cheating lead indirectly to his own death and that of all his magnificent horses. In "The Painted Door" Ann pays for her one act of infidelity with the loss of her husband and a future haunted by her own culpability in his death.

One of the remarkable aspects of nature's indifference is the serene beauty which follows the devastation wrought by hail or blizzard or sandstorm, and which provides an appalling contrast between the indomitable world of nature and the shattered world of humanity. In "A Field of Wheat," when hail destroys John's first good crop after years of struggle against a multitude of natural catastrophes, John and his wife, Martha, see in the wasted fields the beauty and the indomitability of nature.

Nothing but the glitter of sun on hailstones. Nothing but their wheat crushed into little rags of muddy slime. . . . Both of them wanted to speak, to break the atmosphere of calamity that hung over them, but the words they could find were too small for the sparkling serenity of wasted

field. Even as waste it was indomitable. It tethered them to itself, so that
they could not feel or comprehend. It had come and gone, that was all;
before its tremendousness and havoc they were prostrate. They had not yet
risen to cry out or protest.[25]

Their prostration is equivalent to Ann's realization, in "The
Painted Door," of her own puniness in the face of nature. Will, too,
in "September Snow," struggles home to find that the blizzard has
invaded his home, and that his wife is in labor. After his wife's
death he looks out at the day to see in nature, as did John and
Martha, an incredible peace, which contrasts with the violence that
has come and gone leaving death and disaster in its wake:

It was like a spring day, warm and drowsy, with a listless drip from the roof.
In front of him, the oat stacks made a golden splash against the snow.
There was a hushed, breathless silence, as if sky and snow and sunlight
were selfconsciously poised, afraid to wrinkle or dishevel their serenity.
Then through it, a faint, jagged little saw of sound, the baby started to cry.
He felt a twinge of recognition. He seemed to be listening to the same
plaintiveness and protest that had been in Eleanor's voice of late. An impulse seized him to see and hold his baby; but just for a minute longer he
stood there, looking out across the sun-spangled snow, listening. (67)

Here nature is revealed as beautiful but indifferent, serenely uncaring about the havoc it has wrought.
    This passage, however, works in another way as well. The story
ends with the warmth of a spring day although it is September, and
with the sound of a baby's voice; hope and new life are replacing
despair and death. A tiny human voice disturbs the immense
stillness of nature. Margaret Laurence may be referring to this story
when she says, "Hope never quite vanishes. In counterpoint to
desolation runs the theme of renewal."[26] "A Field of Wheat" ends
on a similar note of renewed hope. While Martha realizes her
husband's despair, she sees at the same time his need for her support. And again the beauty of the nature which has ravaged their
land is described in juxtaposition with Martha's renewed strength of
purpose as the story ends:

Withdrawn now in the eastern sky the storm clouds towered, gold-
capped and flushed in the late sunlight, high still pyramids of snowiness
and shadow. And one that Annabelle pointed to, apart, the farthest away of
them all, this one in bronzed slow splendour spread up mountains high to a
vast, plateaulike summit.

Martha hurried inside. She started the fire again, then nailed a blanket over the broken window and lit the big brass parlour lamp—the only one the storm had spared. Her hands were quick and tense. John would need a good supper tonight. The biscuits were water-soaked, but she still had the peas. He liked peas. Lucky that they had picked them when they did. This winter they wouldn't have so much as an onion or potato. (82)

Ross captures in his prose the natural process of death and renewal in nature. Frequently, as in "A Field of Wheat," he indicates a similar process in humanity, as despair is followed by hope and renewed courage. Despite the strong element of determinism in many stories, man's defiance of nature, his persistence despite nature's repeated onslaughts, recalls E. J. Pratt's poems such as "The Truant" and "The Titanic" in which man faces the indifference of nature with stoicism and courage.

VI *Characterization*

The men in Ross's stories are most often physically strong and characterized by dogged endurance. Year after year they cling to the land despite defeat by hail, drought, snow and sand. They say little and rarely express emotion. Their behavior reflects a machismo, a conviction that to show emotion is a weakness, to consider leaving the land a defeat to their manhood.

Reticence, stubbornness and insensitivity are in large measure the causes of the growing rift between these men and their wives. The women appear more imaginative than their husbands insamuch as they see all too clearly the hopelessness of their present struggle and the grim, unending struggle ahead. They are more lonely because more isolated and more helpless, remaining in the house while their men fight the blizzard or storm, or at least, like Paul in "The Lamp at Noon," finding chores to occupy themselves during storm and disaster. Ross's women are often better educated and in many instances, had been more prosperous before marriage; Ellen was a school teacher and her father owned a store; she realizes—as her husband does not—that he is ruining the soil. Will's wife, Eleanor, had completed school and was used to a comfortable home before marriage brought her to his two-room shack, on a farm which even Will knew would never yield more than a meager living. Martha had warned her husband to buy hail insurance, but he ignored her and their crop was destroyed by a hailstorm. These women, seemingly intelligent and prescient, are alienated from husbands who stubbornly resist admission of failure and who avoid emotional expression.

The husband-wife conflict evident in many stories, is introduced in Ross's first published story, "No Other Way." In most of the child-narrated stories the husband-wife conflict is present as an undercurrent, usually stemming from the wife's disappointment with the bleak condition of their lives and her concern that her children seem destined for the same fate. The alienation of the parents in a much later story, "The Flowers that Killed Him" (1972), is a continuation of a theme evident in many child or adolescent-narrated stories including such early ones as "Circus in Town" and "Cornet at Night," written more than thirty years previously.

But Ross's children, not yet concerned with the future, in fact are too caught up with the world of the imagination to be much aware of the drabness of the present. Young Jenny in "Circus in Town" is made as elated by a torn poster of a circus as a child today might be by the circus itself. She does not even consider the possibility of attending the circus itself. Yet, ironically, her mother is upset that they cannot afford the money for the child to attend it. The incident becomes a focus for the mother's resentment at the meagerness of their lives. In "A Day with Pegasus" nine-year-old Peter Parker is borne aloft to another, more exciting world by his new colt and, like Jenny, is yet only vaguely aware of the drabness of the everyday world, from which he has no trouble escaping in his imagination. The thirteen-year-old boy in "The Outlaw" finds excitement and challenge through his horse, Isabel. He and the young boys in "One's a Heifer" and "Cornet at Night" accept unquestioningly the frugality of their lives and find satisfaction in the adult responsibilities which are accorded them.

VII Style and Craft

Ross's humor is gentle and understated. Generally the stories told by children are lighter in tone, thus allowing more opportunities for humor. Realism does not demand of them the same quiet desperation their parents often evince. Children's comments on their parents and their observations on social customs in general are often gently ironic, as the boy's description in "Cornet at Night" of his mother's determined adherence to Sunday ritual and her concern that visitors see that she is "uncontaminated" by her husband's "sacrilege." The same boy's embarrassment at his Sunday corduroys which squeak as if in need of oiling, indicates Ross's understanding of a child's feeling of selfconsciousness at attracting attention. Even "The Flowers that Killed Him," basically a murder story told by a thirteen-year-old, has elements of humor developed through the interaction of the young boys and their relationship with the school principal, the narrator's father.

This last story of Ross indicates his fascination with the criminal mind, a fascination he explores in more detail in later novels. The story differs from earlier ones related by farm boys in the employment of the adolescent voice speaking retrospectively, several days after the final event, rather than the double focus of adult and child. It shares with such stories as "The Painted Door" and "One's a Heifer" the technique of the surprise ending which clarifies much of what has gone before.

Ross is a meticulous craftsman, who reworks his stories and novels to achieve the ultimate effect through precision, economy, and rhythm. He revised all the stories before their republication in *The Lamp at Noon and Other Stories.* A comparison of the early and the revised versions indicates that in most stories revisions involved eliminating adverbs, making minor changes in description of actions, and making slight alterations in dialogue to heighten realism or to modulate rhythm according to the demands of the situation. For example, in the first version of "The Painted Door" Steven says, "There's nothing to be afraid of now, though. I'm going to do the chores for you."[27] In the revised version Steven says "It's all right—nothing to be afraid of. I'm going to see to the stable" (109). The changes are slight, but the clipped, even rhythm of the second version effectively underlines the tense situation in which Steven seeks to soothe the excited woman. Similar minor revisions were made in "A Day with Pegasus" prior to its publication in the collection *Stories from Western Canada.*[28] More extensive changes were made in "Cornet at Night," as indicated earlier, and in "Not by Rain Alone." "Not by Rain Alone" as it appears in *The Lamp at Noon* is composed of two early stories: Part One, subtitled "Summer Thunder," was originally published in *Queen's Quarterly,* Spring 1941, under the title "Not by Rain Alone"; Part Two, "September Snow," had appeared earlier in *Queen's Quarterly,* Winter 1935, under the same title, "September Snow." For consistency the original names of the man and wife in "September Snow," Mark and Ann, were changed to Will and Eleanor (the names of the man and wife in "Not by Rain Alone"). The combination of the two episodes creates a powerful story.

In his descriptive passages Ross often uses words that combine

the suggestive and metaphoric with the concrete, as in this portrayal
of the storm in "The Painted Door":

> The glitter was gone. Across the drifts sped swift and snakelike little
> tongues of snow. She could not follow them, where they sprang from, or
> where they disappeared. It was as if all across the yard the snow were
> shivering awake—roused by the warnings of the wind to hold itself in
> readiness for the impending storm. (105)

Nature comes alive in the personification of snow and wind, and the
Freudian suggestivity of the "snakelike little tongues of snow" adds
to the sexual tension of Ann's situation; connotive diction such as
"warning" and "impending storm" contributes to the tone of anxie-
ty and fear. Ross can, however, just as effectively concentrate on
stark, concrete details with verbs underlining the action, as in this
paragraph describing the awesome power of the hailstorm in "A
Field of Wheat":

> Then the window broke, and Joe and the pillow tumbled off the table
> before the howling inrush of the storm. The stones clattered on the floor
> and bounded up to the ceiling, lit on the stove and threw out sizzling
> steam. The wind whisked pots and kettles off their hooks, tugged at and
> whirled the sodden curtains, crashed down a shelf of lamps and crockery.
> John pushed Martha and Joe into the next room and shut the door. There
> they found Annabelle huddled at the foot of the stairs, round-eyed, biting
> her nails in terror. The window she had been holding was broken too; and
> she had run away without closing the bedroom door, leaving a wild tide of
> wind upstairs to rage unchecked. It was rocking the whole house, straining
> at the walls. Martha ran up to close the door, and came down whimpering.
> (79)

Description at times may be completely suggestive, lacking
specificity yet successfully setting the proper mood: "An early dusk
was closing in. The hush of sun and glare relaxed. A breath of wind
rose furtively, as if released; and the wheat in front of them stood
whispering and cool."[29] The tranquillity of this setting in "Summer
Thunder" mirrors Eleanor's youthful, expectant mood, and, combined with the pleading of the young woman, wins her lover to a
similarly hopeful attitude. Although normally he is a cautious
farmer inclined to wait for the harvest to be in the barn before
building his future on it, he agrees to marry that fall.

Ross's handling of narrative is a major means through which he
reveals the inner worlds of his characters. Through a first-person

point of view or use of a central intelligence, he gets inside the characters to reveal their hopes and fears, dreams and despairs. Thus his impassive and reticent men stand revealed as still determinedly and desperately hopeful for the future, his women all too aware of the drabness of the present, his children serious and dependable, but at the same time imaginative, and excited by their own experiences. By using a double focus in the children's stories Ross can reveal their realistically childish reactions from a mature perspective. His skillful use of landscape to reflect inner reality while the same landscape as outer reality serves as primary antagonist and contributes to mood is one of his most remarkable achievements. This multiple use of landscape is a major factor in the compressed intensity of the stories.

Although Ross professes to be no longer interested in writing short stories, there is no doubt that a number of his stories of prairie farm life, based on his own childhood experiences, are among his best works. In comparison with these, his two army stories, "Jug and Bottle" and "Barrack Room Fiddle Tune" are adequate but unremarkable. "Spike," published in French translation by Pierre Villon in *Liberté* in 1969, has been read on CBC English Radio but was never published in English. This story reverses the usual crime story by revealing the threatening young hitchhiker as a lovelorn young man merely trying to get home to his girl friend on the promised day. This, too, while well crafted, lacks the powerful impact of the prairie stories, in which Ross's tense, compressed style, and his skill at evoking atmosphere and at handling voice all contribute to success.

Despite such generalizations about Ross's stories, an outstanding characteristic of these stories when gathered together is their variety. Stories such as "The Painted Door" and "The Lamp at Noon" are intense, taut, and compressed. "Cornet at Night" and "The Outlaw" are lighter in both tone and texture. "Nell" and "No Other Way" mix comedy with an overridingly somber narrative. Unexpected endings add an extra dimension to "One's a Heifer" and "The Flowers that Killed Him" and an added intensity to "The Painted Door." Common everyday experiences provide the central core of most of the stories. Ross demonstrates his ability to render such experiences significant, to weave out of landscape and prairie farm life patterns of unusual significance.

CHAPTER 3

As For Me and My House

ROSS'S first novel, *As For Me and My House*, is an intense, complex, and ambiguous work which is now recognized as a Canadian classic. In its portrayal of human suffering and struggle, it carries on the realistic tradition of prairie writers of the late 1920's and 1930's. But *As For Me and My House* goes further than any previous work in its revelation of the inner conflict of the protagonists and the tension and complexity of their relationships.

The novel consists of the journal recordings of Mrs. Bentley, a small town minister's wife, from the Bentleys' arrival in Horizon in April to their departure a year later. Characters are few, setting limited, events unremarkable. The novel conveys the atmosphere born of the drought and depression of the 1930's—much the same atmosphere found in Ross's early stories. As with many of the stories, the conflict is a marital one. Much of the impact of the novel comes from the method of its telling. We see everything and everyone from a single perspective, that belonging to Mrs. Bentley. Thus, from the beginning there is an ironic tension created between the words of Mrs. Bentley and the reader's interpretation of these words. Can we accept at face value Mrs. Bentley's explanation of her husband's moods and frustrations? Can we accept her assessment of the townspeople and of the boy, Steve, whom the Bentleys try to adopt, and of Steve's attitude to Philip and Mrs. Bentley? Can we accept her explanations for her own actions and her own attitudes? Her elusiveness is best indicated in our never discovering her first name.

As the novel opens Philip Bentley and his wife are unpacking for the fourth time in twelve years. This is the fourth small town to which Philip has been called to be United Church minister. The Bentleys enter immediately into the role playing aspect of their situation. According to Mrs. Bentley, she is handier with pliers and hammer than Philip, yet she sews curtains while he smashes his fingers opening crates and putting up stove pipes. They play their roles to impress visiting townspeople: "In return for their thousand dollars a year they expect a genteel kind of piety, a well-bred Christianity that will serve as an example to the little sons and daughters of the town."[1] More serious than such minor pretences, as the reader learns at once, is Philip's lack of belief in the religion he preaches and his sense of guilt at his own hypocrisy. In her journal Mrs. Bentley recalls why Philip finds himself in this situation. He is the illegitimate son of a waitress and a young student preacher who died before Philip's birth and was brought up by his mother and her family in a small town much like Horizon. Philip always blamed his mother, who died when he was fourteen, for the ridicule to which his illegitimacy exposed him. When he discovered that his father had wanted to be a painter he resolved to emulate him. At seventeen, to obtain a college education, he accepted an invitation to study for the ministry. Philip's plan was to repay the Church within a few years and then make a vocation of his painting. On graduation, however, he married a young music student. Because of poor appointments, parishioners unable in these years of drought and depression to pay his salary, expenses incurred with the birth of their stillborn child, Philip's debts piled up and he found himself trapped in the small town he had entered the ministry to escape.

Mrs. Bentley senses Philip's growing frustration with his situation and the growing gulf between them. Once, as she says, they had been "partners in conspiracy" against the mean-spirited little towns, but now their own hypocrisy is driving them apart. Now it is "not enough to put a false front up and live our own lives out behind it" (16). A major difference between herself and her husband, as Mrs. Bentley sees it, is that her own failure, in being a small town preacher's wife instead of the musician she once aspired to be, is not important to her because she is in love with Philip. Her husband, however, is bitter at the failure of finding himself, after twelve years, still a small town preacher who doesn't believe his own words, rather than being the artist he once dreamed of becoming.

As Philip feels guilty at living a lie, Mrs. Bentley now feels increasingly guilty for her part in keeping Philip from realizing his role as an artist, for having won him to marriage through her music. Realizing the effect on their marriage of Philip's growing frustration, Mrs. Bentley determines to act. She suggests adopting twelve-year-old Steve whose father has deserted him. The boy gives

Philip's life new purpose. When the boy is taken away, Philip again becomes bitter and resentful. He reacts by having a brief affair with a young choir member, Judith West, an outsider herself who has become a friend of Mrs. Bentley. Unknown to Philip, his wife is aware of his adultery; desperate to save their marriage, she suggests adopting Judith's baby. Judith conveniently dies. At the novel's end Mrs. Bentley reveals to Philip that she knew the child was his, thus eliminating a barrier of deception between them. By this time the Bentleys have enough money to leave Horizon and start a new life in the city, where Philip will operate a second-hand book store and, it is hoped, return to his painting, free of the hypocrisy and sense of guilt that have haunted his life as a minister.

I   Mrs. Bentley's Journal

Sinclair Ross tells us that originally he intended this novel to be the story of Philip narrated by his wife, who would be in a position to reveal him more perceptively and honestly than could Philip himself.[2] However, as the author himself admits, Mrs. Bentley became more central than her creator had anticipated. In fact, the narrative acts in two directions: outwardly to reveal Philip, a simple, stark actor in the drama, and inwardly to reveal Mrs. Bentley, a complex, sensitive sharer in the action as well as Philip's reporter and interpreter. As writer of the journal, Mrs. Bentley is an eyewitness narrator who records events almost as they occur. There is an ironic gap between the narrator and the reader as the reader attempts to establish the accuracy of Mrs. Bentley's assumptions and of her interpretations of others' behavior and, indeed, of her own motives and actions. There is also an ironic gap between Mrs. Bentley and her husband, who says little, preferring to avoid emotional scenes by often walking white-lipped into his study, shutting the door behind him. Although she believes she understands Philip, there are a number of incidents recounted in Mrs. Bentley's journal which clearly indicate that she does not; for example, although she claims that Philip does not like to show his paintings to others, he does, as we see, display an interest in others' reactions to his paintings on several occasions.

In this novel, then, there exists a divided protagonist formed of the eyewitness narrator and sharer in the action, Mrs. Bentley, and the central actor in the novel, Philip Bentley. The development of Mrs. Bentley as observer far beyond her original role is reminiscent of Henry James's development of the observer, Strether, in *The Ambassadors* who is, as Wayne Booth notes, "a revealing instance of James's tendency to develop an observer far beyond his original function."[3] The most basic source of ambiguity and irony in the novel resides in Mrs. Bentley, whose role and personality have intrigued most critics of *As For Me and My House.*

Ross controls the reader's impressions through his use of the single perspective. It is Mrs. Bentley's view of the landscape, the town, the townspeople, the farmers in the outlying mission, and of herself and her husband which is conveyed to the reader, and it must always be subjected by the reader to careful scrutiny. Because she is writing of herself and of her own experiences and attitudes, of her husband and her attempts to reach him, her narrative is intensely subjective; there is no attempt on her part to step back and view the situation or herself dispassionately. Mrs. Bentley thus is not a reliable narrator; she is sufficiently dependable that we may accept her reports of actual events, but we must be aware that her interpretation of these events, and her selection of the details to report and those to omit, will influence our ability to interpret the episodes and those involved in them. Insofar as Philip, Judith, Paul, and the townspeople are concerned, we must view Mrs. Bentley's interpretations of their behavior and motives with some suspicion. When she is inaccurate in her assumptions or conclusions she is self-deceiving as well as deceiving of the reader. She does not realize her own errors, although she does later admit the error of some of her judgments, but only when she has been clearly demonstrated to be wrong. A complex irony evolves from this perspective.

Since she is writing a diary, Mrs. Bentley is using the confessional mode; she is, in effect, talking to herself. One reason she writes is to give voice to her feelings. Her journal is born partly of her loneliness, of having no one in whom she can confide. She cannot talk freely to her husband—at least she feels she cannot. The first day in Horizon she mentions how careful she must be not to reveal her true feelings to him: "I ran my fingers through his hair, then stooped and kissed him. Lightly, for that is of all things what I mustn't do, let him ever suspect me of being sorry"(4). In writing her journal Mrs. Bentley reviews in her own mind the incidents which seem to her of most importance in her day-to-day life—incidents involving her relationship with her husband and theirs with the town. She explores her own feelings and reactions to events and people, and ponders what she should do.

Mrs. Bentley does not write a daily—or in any way a regular—report of events. She may write four or five times a week, then be silent two to three weeks. She may then write a lengthy account or a brief note. We assume that she writes in more detail of those conversations or incidents which most disturb or preoccupy her, less of those she considers of minor significance. Much is omitted altogether. Her own musings and reflections, her self-doubts and private fears are often recorded. These help the reader to interpret her personality and attitude.

The dates on which Mrs. Bentley writes are clustered around several incidents central to the Bentleys' Horizon experience. Her first evening in Horizon Mrs. Bentley writes of her impressions of the move to this little town. During the first couple of months she reports events and records opinions three to four times weekly—noting her own and her husband's response to the townspeople, their growing friendship with Paul Kirby and Judith West, and their adoption of Steve. Frequent entries occur in her journal once again on return to Horizon from their holiday at the ranch, as the changed scene enables her to view her marriage and their position in town from a new perspective. After her discovery in August of Judith's affair with Philip—only four months after their arrival in Horizon, but three-fourths of the way through the novel—entries are scattered, tapering off to once a week or less, until April. The main events in the Bentley experience of Horizon occur within the first four months, April to August. With the birth of Judith's baby in April there are several entries, and the final note in the journal is made on the Bentleys' last day in Horizon in May. Counterpointing Mrs. Bentley's account of incidents and their repercussions is her description of wind, drought, and rain, as the novel moves through the cycle of the seasons from spring through summer, fall, and winter to the following spring.

Mrs. Bentley writes in the evening, as the heading of each entry indicates. The time is appropriate. Evening is the hour when a Christian examines his conscience, reviewing his activities, in order to make an honest assessment of himself and to determine upon his behavior for the future. Evening suggests also Mrs. Bentley's loneliness. The work of the day completed, most couples spend these moments together, recounting the day's events, exchanging confidences, discussing problems, planning their future. For the Bentleys, the situation is notably different. Mrs. Bentley sits alone writing her journal, brooding over her life and her marriage, while in parallel fashion, her husband sits alone in his study, voicing his reactions to his life in his sketches, the door between them closed.

The journal form lends itself to the subjective, introspective contemplation of events. The reader, like an eavesdropper, is privy to emotions and thoughts which the writer is not prepared to share, even with her husband or friends. The initial tendency of the reader of a first-person narrative is to identify and sympathize with the narrator, as his interest becomes engaged with her actions and reactions.

The novel rewards frequent rereading. Because of the complex irony involved, additional subtle nuances and hints at different interpretations of events and personalities are revealed with each reading. Added to the subtlety of the point of view are the intensity and compression of the narrative, which create an effect akin to poetry. The evocation of mood through weather—wind, dust, drought—and constant mirroring of the Bentleys' inner states through climate and surroundings and through other characters, contribute to the intensity. Only a week after their arrival Mrs. Bentley realizes that the town is a mirror of herself: "And the little town outside was somehow too much like a mirror. Or better, like a whole set of mirrors. Ranged round me so that at every step I met the preacher's wife, splayfooted rubbers, dowdy coat and all. I couldn't escape. The gates and doors and windows kept reminding me"(23). This mirror motif remains paramount in the novel.

Throughout this richly textured work details of setting reveal Mrs. Bentley's situation; her own impressionistic description becomes an unconscious revelation of fears and emotions of which she herself is only vaguely aware, and the sources of which she does not seem to know. For example, Mrs. Bentley's first description of the town is heavily symbolical once the reader realizes that, as Mrs. Bentley says, the town is a mirror of herself: "The town seems huddled together, cowering on a high, tiny perch, afraid to move lest it topple into the wind. Close to the parsonage is the church, black even against the darkness, towering ominously up through the night and merging with it. There's a soft steady swish of rain on the roof, and a gurgle of eave troughs running over. Above, in the high cold night, the wind goes swinging past, indifferent, liplessly mournful. It frightens me, makes me feel lost, dropped on this little perch of town and abandoned"(5). The Bentleys themselves in this new town are "huddled together,"; they are "cowering on a high tiny perch afraid to move," that is, they are walking a tightrope of pretence by preaching a religion they do not believe, fearful of losing their means of livelihood if they deviate from the watchful town's expectations in appearance, attitude, or behavior: the wind, as we see later, is life itself which the Bentleys are afraid to face, which one false step in the town can propel them into facing. The church towers "ominously" over the parsonage, their house, as it does over their lives, and the "indifferent," "mournful" wind swings past as life itself goes on without them, leaving her feeling "lost" and "abandoned."

Of the false fronts on the buildings in Philip's drawings, Mrs. Bentley says, "The false fronts haven't seen the prairie. Instead they stare at each other across the street as into mirrors of themselves, absorbed in their own reflections" (69), just as she and Philip behind their own false fronts stare into themselves, absorbed in themselves.

The repression of emotion and the sexual tension in the Bentley marriage are projected onto the house, the town, and the weather, and assault all the senses. The pervasive musty smell of the house seems "a passive, clinging" one, with a "vague suggestion of musty shelves, repression, and decay" which she describes time after time as a "faint exhalation of the past" (13). By August the mustiness seems to be getting thicker as the oppressiveness of their marital relationship, which the Bentleys cannot resolve or shake off, intensifies. It is their house after all, which this smell pervades and, as the title of the novel makes clear, their "house" means their family, their marriage. The "sly, crafty-looking windows" and the feeling of something lurking in the shadows add to the oppressive atmosphere and reflect the sense of guilt of the hypocrite who must always fear discovery. The passive, clinging smell, the oppressive house, the town like a mirror, the dust and lurking shadows—all create a claustrophobic setting.

As the novel itself takes two directions, operating outwardly to focus on Philip as seen through his wife's eyes and inwardly to reveal Mrs. Bentley, so also the tension and irony in the novel operate in two directions. From the beginning, the Bentleys are in conflict with the town. Their life in Horizon is a constant pretence—preaching what they do not believe, acting outwardly as the town would wish them to act while inwardly rebelling, putting up a false front to their parishioners and their neighbors. Feeling guilty and therefore feeling constantly watched, they see everywhere projections of their own feelings of guilt and repression.

This is the exterior tension created by the situation of the Bentleys versus the town. But there is a deeper underlying tension between Philip Bentley and his wife, people who mask their true feelings. The word "pretence" occurs time after time in Mrs. Bentley's journal. Mrs. Bentley "pretends" to be asleep when her husband comes to bed, and vice versa. When Mrs. Bentley suggests to Philip he visit the pregnant Judith, he "pretends" it is too cold to ride there on horseback and she "pretends" to believe him. Even after she has flung the truth at Philip, thus removing the major obstacle to honesty remaining between them, he "pretends" to be asleep when she goes into the bedroom and she "pretends" she believes he is asleep. Mrs. Bentley differs from her husband in continuing to accept hypocrisy as a way of life, whereas he has become disgusted with it and finds this acceptance objectionable in her.

Because of Philip Bentley's reticence, Mrs. Bentley's ability to report his remarks and reactions is severely limited. Ross's portrayal of Philip as an artist was a brilliant conception, for the silent Philip can be interpreted by the reader through his sketches, much as his wife can be understood through her diary. The complexity of the work has to do with these means of revelation. Mrs. Bentley is unaware of how much she divulges of herself in her diary, especially in her description of the town, the landscape and the weather. But, also, she is aware only occasionally, and to a limited extent, of Philip's disclosure of himself through his sketches and paintings. Ross reveals both the Bentleys to the observant reader through their two art forms—writing and painting.

II   *Nature and the Cosmos*

Man's dilemma in an indifferent universe is a central theme of the novel, ironically captured in this story of a minister and his wife neither of whom believes in the religion they represent. The setting which reflects their moods also conveys their sensation of being lost in an indifferent universe. From the beginning wind and rain convey the indifference of nature, and the town's huddled houses are projections of Mrs. Bentley's own feelings of helplessness in the face of cosmic indifference. On her first day in Horizon she notes in her journal: "Above, in the high cold night, the wind goes swinging past, indifferent, liplessly mournful. It frightens me, makes me feel lost, dropped on this little perch of town and abandoned" (5).

Mrs. Bentley's longing for faith is indicated by her thoughts as she walks alone outside the town on Christmas Eve. Horizon appears to her "a rocky, treacherous island," and as she reflects on the beauty around her she wishes, "that on such an unearthly, radiant night I might be a little less of a rationalist, able to feel the ecstasy of Christmas" (148). In her frequent evening walks, the prairie itself reinforces her sensation of being lost: "When you pause a moment to look across the prairie a queer, lost sensation comes over you of being hung aloft in space, so like a floor of clouds does the unbroken whiteness coil and swell to the horizon" (150). The town, which itself appears to her to be lost on the prairie, is a projection of Mrs. Bentley's own situation. Like the snow, dust obscures her vision, creating the same impression of empty space ahead of her: "The dust is so thick that sky and earth are just a blur. You can scarcely see the elevators at the end of town. One step beyond, you think, and you'd go plunging into space" (73). As in Ross's later novel, *The Well*, space is on one level the unknown future. The Bentleys fear plunging into the unknown by leaving the little town and the safety of their lives here. On another level space is, for the agnostic Bentleys, that vast unknown beyond life itself.

Of the drought-ridden farmers who attend the country mission services Mrs. Bentley says, "Five years in succession now they've been blown out, dried out, hailed out; and it was as if in the face of so blind and uncaring a universe they were trying to assert themselves, to insist upon their own meaning and importance" (19). Paul, who is, like Mrs. Bentley, a rationalist, explains their religious faith as a means whereby man tries to find some source of comfort in a "blind and uncaring universe":

Man can't bear to admit his insignificance. If you've ever seen a hailstorm, or watched a crop dry up—his helplessness, the way he's ignored—well, it was just such helplessness in the beginning that set him discovering gods who could control the storms and seasons. Powerful, friendly gods—on his side. And if they were more powerful than the storms, and if they were concerned with him above all things, then it followed that he was really more powerful and important than the storms, too. So he felt better—gratefully became a reverent and religious creature. That was what you heard this morning—pagans singing Christian hymns . . . *pagan*, you know, originally that's exactly what it meant, *country dweller*. (19)

Paul is explaining the religious faith of the farmers who attend the mission services each week. A man who has faith, as Paul explains, has some consolation for the trials he must undergo. But for the

Bentleys, who do not believe, there is no such consolation. They are only too aware of man's insignificance, of his helplessness in the face of hail and drought, of the "blind and uncaring" universe, and of their own dilemma, beset by disappointments and frustrations in this narrow restrictive town.

III A Surrogate Son

Soon after the Bentleys' arrival in Horizon they are provided with the opportunity to have the son for which Philip has always longed. Steve, son of an Eastern European immigrant, is deserted by his father. Mrs. Bentley admits that a major reason why she suggests taking Steve is her sense of guilt at not having borne Philip a son. Their one child was stillborn the first year of their marriage: as a result she has carried a burden of guilt through the past twelve years. She feels that Philip's marriage to her, which has impeded his first ambition to become an artist, should at least have brought him fulfillment of his second wish, to have a son. By failing to bear him a son she considers herself responsible for disappointing this ambition, too.

Ironically, Steve does little to bring the Bentleys together. Despite her eagerness to stir Philip out of his apathy, Mrs. Bentley discovers that she is jealous of his attention to the boy. At their first meeting with Steve, she comments: "I didn't look at Steve or Philip now, but I could feel them standing there, unaware of us, complete for the moment in themselves. I don't know what came over me—maybe just the wind, the plaintive way it whined. I seemed to feel myself vaguely threatened" (42). Again, at supper the same evening Mrs. Bentley admits: "Steve was on my mind. There was something rankling in me that my reason couldn't justify" (42).

When, one week later, Steve's father leaves town and the Bentleys decide to take the boy, the prospect of having a son produces an instant effect on Philip. Mrs. Bentley describes the change: "This unexpected advent of a son, I must admit, has brought a little life and enthusiasm to his face, taken some of the sag out of his shoulders. He kept pacing up and down when he was out here, and his step for the first time in years had a ring. There was eagerness and vitality radiating from him to make me aware how young he still is, how handsome and tall and broad-shouldered. Which if it lasts is going to make things harder still, I'm afraid, seeing that Steve hasn't rejuvenated me, too" (50 - 51).

Mrs. Bentley's attitude to Steve at this time scarcely appears loving. When she fixes up the lean-to shed behind the kitchen as his bedroom, Philip resents the meager accommodation she is providing for the boy, "as if I were trying to put him out of the way" (51). His resentment compels her at least to take the woodbox, broom, mop, and dusters out of the shed and put curtains on the windows. The day Steve moves into their house, Mrs. Bentley confesses her ambivalent feelings toward him: "I like Steve, and at the same time I resent him. I grudge every minute he and Philip are alone together" (52). When Philip takes Steve to the country on his calls and clearly does not want her along, she is amazed at her emotional reaction. But her outburst causes her to acknowledge her possessive attitude, to admit that she has been wrong in trying to possess Philip, and that she has never succeeded in doing so anyway. Now she recognizes the closed study door as a symbol of Philip's refusal to be possessed: "He worked on stubbornly with his chalk and pencil, intent on his drawings that with every year became a little colder and grimmer. Partly because he was an artist, because he had to draw; partly because he was a man, and the solitude of his study was his last stronghold against me" (64). Finally, she sees that she has not lost Philip to Steve, for as she admits, "He was never really mine to lose to anyone" (64).

An incident at Sunday School in which Mrs. Bentley and Philip together defend Steve against Mrs. Finley seems, to Mrs. Bentley, to unite them momentarily. Philip is almost pushed to action and now his wife thinks, "If he were to break away now it might mean worry and hardship, but it might also mean getting a fresh grip of himself, recovering something of his old independence and ambition. Especially now that there are the three of us" (67). Appropriately, at this time her garden starts to grow, despite the dust and drought. These days seem to be the most hopeful in Mrs. Bentley's Horizon experience. Her own dried up emotions begin to function, and of her newly developing affection for Steve she says, "I didn't know anything like that could happen to me. It was as if once, twelve years ago, I had heard the beginning of a piece of music, and then a door had closed. But within me, in my mind and blood, the music had kept on, and when at last they opened the door again I was at the right place, had held the rhythm all the way" (69). Yet, even now, when Philip, impelled by his sense of responsibility to this new son, writes to his former ministries requesting payment of back salary, she reacts once more with jealousy and resentment, because he had never made such an effort for her sake. Before the Bentleys begin their July holiday the drought has once again overcome the land, her garden is slowly dying, and even with Steve present the tension between the Bentleys continues. Through Steve, Mrs. Bentley has been forced to admit her possessiveness. She writes on June 6:

I must still keep on reaching out, trying to possess him, trying to make myself matter. I must, for I've left myself nothing else. I haven't been like him. I've reserved no retreat, no world of my own. I've whittled myself hollow that I might enclose and hold him, and when he shakes me off I'm just a shell. Ever since the day he let me see I was less to him than Steve I've been trying to find and live my own life again, but it's empty, unreal. The piano, even—I try, but it's just a tinkle. And that's why I mustn't admit I may have lost him. He's spoiling Steve, hurting him, and I must stand by and let him. He would resent my interference. It would make me one with the town then, hostile, critical, aligned against him. He would resent and even hate me if I did, and I'm too small for that, too cowardly. (75)

As her journal entries at this time indicate, Mrs. Bentley has come to some self-awareness through Steve's presence, through the emotions he stirs within her. For Mrs. Bentley, after twelve years in the repressive environment of these little towns and twelve years of singleminded devotion to possessing Philip, has become as she indicates, as dried up emotionally as her little garden. Her term "I'm just a shell" is not inappropriate. Ironically, her description of Philip in terms of dried up flowers is really an equally apt description for herself, ". . . bursting in after him I put my arms around his middle before he could sit down and hung on tight. He tried to laugh, but the sound curled up on him the same way my sick little poppy and nasturtium leaves curl up against the blistered earth" (79).

IV *The Ranch*

On the invitation of Paul Kirby, the Bentleys spend their two-week July holiday at the ranch of Paul's brother, Stanley. The ranch episode, situated midway through the novel, functions in several ways to bring the Bentleys closer to a resolution of their dilemma. The locale itself suggests an opening out, in contrast to the repression and entrapment of Horizon. As they drive toward the ranch Mrs. Bentley notes: "And there's a cowboy once who waves as we pass, and whose solitary figure against the horizon gives the landscape for a moment vastness that we hadn't felt before" (92). The flowing river also suggests life and vigor. Steve, Paul, and Philip camp on the river bank. Throughout the two-week holiday, they are far from the stultifying small town atmosphere. Here Philip becomes engrossed in his paintings, and his sketches indicate that he is being affected by his proximity to external nature. He mellows sufficiently to spend his last two days painting Laura's stallion, which for Laura is a symbol of the excitement and passion missing in her life.

Shortly after their arrival, Mrs. Bentley notes her own reaction to the landscape; she contrasts her sense of uneasiness here, her fear of the wilderness, with the very different, self-sufficient atmosphere of Horizon:

We've all lived in a little town too long. The wilderness here makes us uneasy. I felt it first the night I walked alone along the river bank—a queer sense of something cold and fearful, something inanimate, yet aware of us. A Main Street is such a self-sufficient little pocket of existence, so smug, compact, that here we feel abashed somehow before the hills, their passiveness, the unheeding way they sleep. We climb them, but they withstand us, remain as serene and unrevealed as ever. The river slips past, unperturbed by our coming and going, stealthily confident. We shrink from our insignificance. (99 - 100).

Although Mrs. Bentley uses the plural "we," she is, in fact, recording her own reaction to the landscape. It is she who is fearful walking along the river, not Philip or Steve or Paul who cheerfully camp by the river while she remains indoors. It is she whom the hills and river, "the wilderness" as she says, makes uneasy and causes to "shrink from [her] insignificance." Philip, on the contrary, spends the days along the river bank sketching and painting. He does not demonstrate the terror of nature and the wilderness which mrs. Bentley evinces when she says: "The close black hills, the stealthily slipping sound the river made—it was as if I were entering dead, forbidden country, approaching the lair of the terror that destroyed the hills, that was lurking there still among the skulls" (95). Philip, with Steve and Paul, sits by their campfire at the river's edge while Mrs. Bentley recounts how she flees to her small, stuffy room, where the pictures of pure-bred bulls and stallions on her walls fittingly suggest her rejection of natural life and vigor for the artificial, the role of participant for that of voyeur.

Stanley's wife, Laura, spends much of her time with Mrs.

Bentley, and her frank observations compel Mrs. Bentley to see the extent to which she herself has taken on small town mannerisms and attitudes: and that she is becoming, in fact, what she has pretended to be. Mrs. Bentley is hurt by Laura's ridicule: "In front of the cowboys at noon today she mimicked me at a Ladies Aid meeting leading in prayer. Some of them in Horizon are just as critical and venomous, but they work with more finesse. The needle's in before you know it. It's easier to maintain face" (95). But Mrs. Bentley admits catching herself sounding like the small town preacher's wife: "I speak or laugh, and suddenly in my voice catch a hint of the benediction. It just means, I suppose, that all these years the Horizons have been working their will on me. My heresy, perhaps, is less than I sometimes think" (93). At the small town dance the Bentleys attend with Laura and Steve, Mrs. Bentley again sees that she is behaving as a Horizon matron: "But for a long time I sat out of it, more Horizon-minded, I suppose, than sometimes I admit" (96). But as she sits thinking of Horizon, she finds herself caught up in the excitement of this new, open and hopeful town whose life is symbolized by the music: "But while I sat philosophizing the heyday, mushroom town was there; and gradually the Horizon matron slipped away from me, and before I knew it my foot had started tapping with the music too" (97).

This holiday experience allows Mrs. Bentley to see herself more clearly as "more Horizon-minded" than she had realized, and to accept her responsibility for making Philip what he is. On her return to town, she can say, "For these last twelve years I've kept him in the Church—no one else. The least I can do now is help get him out again" (107). This conclusion brings her a determination to save the money which their former parishes have been sending so that they can leave Horizon and Philip can be freed from the ministry:

Things haven't been the same since our two weeks on the ranch. Horizon was always bad enough. Now it's simply out of the question.

Without knowing it we relaxed a little out there, looked back and saw ourselves. Maybe Laura helped us. We didn't like it when she sneered, but she was right. We said to ourselves, she was just loud and common, but she saw us pretty well for what we are. She was honest when she looked at Philip and said it seemed a pity. (107)

Once again, as when she spoke of her fear of nature, Mrs. Bentley uses the pronoun "we." The reader cannot be sure she is right to speak for her husband as well as herself with: "We looked back and saw ourselves" and, "We didn't like it when she sneered." The incidents during the holiday which Mrs. Bentley has described in her journal suggest that she herself has looked back and seen herself more clearly. Her acceptance now of her responsibility for keeping Philip in the church confirms this.

V *Judith*

Judith and Paul, the two outsiders whom the Bentleys meet their first Sunday in Horizon, provide complicating factors in the Bentleys' lives and initiate events which lead the Bentleys out of their own hypocrisy and out of the repressed, hypocritical world of the small prairie town.

The words Mrs. Bentley uses to describe her first·impression of Judith West are "sensitive" and "white." The sensitivity and the whiteness both suggest to the reader an affinity with Philip, the sensitive, white-lipped artist. Yet strangely Mrs. Bentley, who admits that in every new church she looks up and down the aisle, "frightened, a little primitive, green-eyed," for anyone she suspects may become a threat to her marriage, does not view Judith as a threat. The first night they meet the shy young choir member, Mrs. Bentley can say: "Not that there was anyone tonight. After the congregation had gone we sat a few minutes getting acquainted with the choir, and it would have taken an imagination livelier even than mine to find much to be afraid of there" (10).

From time to time Judith drops in to listen to Mrs. Bentley playing the piano or to have supper with the Bentleys. As they become friends she shares with Mrs. Bentley her hopes for the future. The depression has affected her dreams too. As a young farm girl she worked in the fields like a man, stooking hay and driving a binder to earn money for a commercial course. This was to be her means of escape into a fuller life. But on graduation she was unable to find a job in the city. Now she is working for a Horizon family. In town she feels she is one step nearer the city to which she is determined to make her way eventually. She could have taken the easier way of marriage to a successful neighboring farmer, but instead continues to fight for an opportunity to have her own career, to express herself. Judith is linked with nature by her background and with art by her remarkable voice.

Philip and Judith are alike in other ways besides their sensitivity and whiteness. Both are quietly determined. Both long to escape the bleak prairie towns. Like Philip in his boyhood, Judith used to go down to the station to watch the trains come and go, symbols of escape into a larger world, a world of opportunity. Like both the Bentleys, Judith's longing for a different life sets her apart from the townspeople. Her music also indicates that, like the Bentleys, she too is an artist. Her affinity with Philip is greater, however, he continues his sketching—as she continues her singing—whereas his wife has long ago given up her dream of a musical career for marriage. She and Philip are similar in their quiet determination. Both keep some private inner area secure from the prying town and, as Philip suggests with his tight-lipped silence and closed study door, secure from possessive wives as well.

Philip's interest in Judith at their first meeting is first indicated by his desire to capture her on paper. Only three weeks later their strong mutual attraction becomes obvious. This attraction is also augmented through another art—music, her singing. The strength of Judith's personality and her courage in facing life are indicated by the manner in which her voice conquers the wind:

> The wind was too strong for Philip or the choir, but Judith scaled it when she sang alone again before the closing hymn.
> The rest of us, I think, were vaguely and secretly a little afraid. The strum and whimper were wearing on our nerves. But Judith seemed to respond to it, ride up with it, feel it the way a singer feels an orchestra. There was something feral in her voice, that even the pace and staidness of her hymn could not restrain.
> "She stood there all the time so white and small," Philip said afterwards. "Unaware of herself."
> It's seldom he listens to music, but as soon as she began tonight he turned in his chair behind the pulpit and sat with his eyes fixed on her all the way through the hymn. I could see him in the little mirror over the organ that's there for the organist to watch the progress of the collection plate, and know when it's time to taper off the offertory. Even after she had finished he sat a few minutes without stirring. There was an uneasy clearing of throats and rustling of hymn books as the congregation waited for him. (38)

Mrs. Bentley's obtuseness is evident when, after making these observations, she invites Judith home and fails to see why the girl appeared "too self-conscious to talk, and after an uncomfortable half-hour stood up suddenly, and said Mrs. Wenderby would be wanting her for the children" (39). Nor can Mrs. Bentley see why, once Judith had left, Philip paces restlessly up and down, then goes to his study and closes the door. Mrs. Bentley interprets his actions as "a pity for me, a regret for the way things stood between us, a helplessness to do anything about it" (39), and adds "Not that things between us tonight are much different from any other night." Mrs. Bentley is wrong. Things are different; from this time Philip and Judith are aware of their attraction for one another. Through Mrs. Bentley's report of events, Ross subtly reveals to the perceptive reader both the growing attraction between Philip and Judith and Mrs. Bentley's strange lack of awareness of this attraction.

The fact that Judith withstands the wind which defeats everyone else, as noted in the preceding passage, is an indication of her strength. As she admits to Mrs. Bentley, she is not a coward for something she wants. She is not afraid of life. Two months later, when Mrs. Bentley finally does perceive the attraction between her husband and Judith which is obvious to the reader of her diary from the account of their first meeting, she shows that she herself appreciates the hidden strength of the young girl. In an apt image, she contrasts Judith's strength with rushing water which moves so swiftly it seems "still, solid like glass." Yet she does not seem to realize that the image she uses suggests passion as well as quiet strength; nor does she realize that Judith understands her own feelings for Philip:

She doesn't know yet. I wish I could spare her the day she must find out. For behind the white face and timid eyes there's something fearless, a press of strong, untried womanhood. It's just like the day Philip and I sat in the snowstorm watching the water rush through the stones—so swift that sometimes, as we watched, it seemed still, solid like glass. I've looked at her sometimes, slight, self-conscious, irresolute, and wondered at the will and strength it must have taken to resist her family and leave the farm. . . . She's going to find there are harder things than driving a grain team or stooking in the harvest field. (91 - 92)

Mrs. Bentley is more prophetic than she realizes with her last remark, "She's going to find there are harder things than driving a grain team or stooking in the harvest field." Judith dies in childbirth, refusing to name the father of her child. Judith's mother, who believes that her daughter has disgraced the family, ironically says to Mrs. Bentley, "You and your husband are good people. You're real Christians, and I'm glad you're taking the baby" (161), while

Mrs. Bentley confesses, "For me it's easier this way. It's what I've secretly been hoping for all along. I'm glad she's gone—glad—for her sake as much as ours. What was there ahead of her now anyway?" (161 - 162). Judith, who hoped to have enough money saved to escape Horizon in the spring, does that spring escape in a sense, but not to a fulfillment of any of her dreams.

VI *Paul*

Ross's development of the relationship of Paul Kirby with Mrs. Bentley parallels the Judith-Philip affair. Mrs. Bentley's friendship with the young schoolteacher is more complex than she knows or admits in her journal. Paul, like the Bentleys, is an outsider. Because of his education he no longer belongs on the ranch, yet he is not comfortable in town. He is a serious young man caught up with the meanings and sources of words, a preoccupation which links him with the problem of communication which pervades the novel.

It soon becomes apparent—to Philip if not to Mrs. Bentley—that it is she Paul is interested in visiting. Not long after their initial meeting he appears in cowboy clothes (including a big sombrero and a bright red-spotted handkerchief) to show Mrs. Bentley his horse; and a few weeks later appears again for his weekly drive to the Sunday mission with the Bentleys, wearing a new suit, tan shoes, and a fedora, looking, as Mrs. Bentley says, "like a farmer at a picnic in his Sunday best." Mrs. Bentley reports these events but makes no attempt to account for them.

Paul's proprietary attitude to Mrs. Bentley becomes obvious at the ranch. At a dance in the nearby town, Mrs. Bentley accepts the invitation of a strange young cowboy for supper and a stroll through town, admitting that her behavior is motivated by the desire to make Philip jealous. But it is Paul who reacts: "A puritanical corner of his modern young mind in ascendancy for the moment, he told me roundly I should have had more sense. After a long, celibate week on the range just what did I think brought the cowboys to town on Saturday night? It was especially bad being asked to go and see a horse" (98). Paul's behavior contrasts with that of Philip, who "nodded good-humoredly each time we danced past, a faint twist to his lips, as if he thought my stripling cowboy funny. I hoped he would resent him, but he didn't" (98). Strangely, Mrs. Bentley, in recording this incident, does not see the significance in Paul's response; he is demonstrating the jealousy she had hoped to arouse in her husband. Conversely, Philip's look of amusement indicates only pleasure that she has, at least momentarily, cast off the role of Horizon matron. Mrs. Bentley also fails to see that Philip has more cause for jealousy of her developing relationship with Paul than of her brief interlude with a young stranger at a dance.

To the reader it is not surprising that Philip's jealousy becomes overt on Paul's return from the two-month school holiday. The first time Paul visits the Bentleys after their ranch holiday, Philip makes an excuse to leave—ostensibly for·a few minutes—and stays away for nearly two hours. Mrs. Bentley does not appear to see that this behavior is an indication of his displeasure. While Philip is away, she takes Paul into Philip's study to view his paintings; her report that when Philip returned "he caught us there" suggests a sense of guilt on her part. To make matters worse, when Paul leaves that evening, Mrs. Bentley decides to go for a walk. Philip's assumption that she has gone with Paul and his suspicions of her explanation seem reasonable to the reader.

If Mrs. Bentley does not understand what is happening, at least Paul does. He sees both Philip's jealousy and resentment and his own growing affection for Mrs. Bentley. Mrs. Bentley, in reporting various incidents involving Paul, seems blissfully unaware: " 'What's wrong with Paul these days, he never comes round,' I said to Philip, and over his shoulder he withered me, 'I'd say yhat that's one for you to answer' " (132). A few days after this exchange, he responds to her casual mention of Paul with, "Things are patched up between you then?" Mrs. Bentley's only reply is "a stony look of superiority," obviously implying that his jealousy is beyond notice. Not long after, Mrs. Bentley contrasts Philip's ineptitude with Paul's capability. Philip's angry reaction, "Why not get your mind off Paul, and remember you're a married woman?" (134), sparks an equally angry reaction from her. Yet she can persuade herself that Philip is not jealous and has nothing to be jealous of: "Thinking it over now I know he didn't really mean anything when he spoke of Paul" (134). Mrs. Bentley thus consistently misjudges both Paul's feelings for her and Philip's interpretation of her relationship with Paul.

Ross links the two romantic entanglements in a situation in which neither party is guilty but each suspects the other. While Philip visits a dying man, his wife suspiciously goes to the Wenderby house to try to discover whether he is secretly meeting Judith.

When Mrs. Bentley arrives home covered with snow, having found that her fears were groundless, she excitedly denies having been with Paul before such an accusation is made, thus persuading Philip of her guilt.

The culmination of this series of incidents involving Philip's growing anger at his wife's behavior with Paul occurs at the Ladies Aid play in September. Mrs. Bentley plays the same Liszt rhapsody with which she had won Philip years earlier. Although she has planned this for Philip, he, not surprisingly given the accumulated tensions and his suspicions up to this time, berates her for using her music to win Paul: " 'Your success tonight.' His voice began to shake itself out, louder and harsher. 'After all your practicing—it would have been a pity if it had gone to waste. I thought the poor fool was going to prostrate himself'" (145).

Finally in April Mrs. Bentley is forced to admit Paul's love for her:

> I walked up the railroad track this afternoon as far as the ravine with Paul. He was on his way home from school just as I was starting out. He said if I didn't mind he'd come too, and then all the way there and back was silent.
>
> I'd never thought of him like that before, but there was such a strained, helpless look in his eyes that suddenly I felt the windows all accusing me. Somehow it seemed that they all must know now, too. I couldn't refuse him, but I was such a coward I walked in misery till we had left the town behind. All the time I had thought it was only Philip, something he was trying to imagine. Paul had been silent with me often before, thoughtful, masculine, self-sufficient silences, but this time it was just a helpless, numb one of awareness, like a woman's, and I could tell by it that he was suffering.
>
> I kept silent too. It seemed strange that I now should make another suffer who had suffered so much that way myself. (158)

It is worth noting that, once she recognizes Paul's love for her, Mrs. Bentley begins to feel differently about him; she confesses an attachment she had never allowed herself to admit before. Commenting on her reliance upon Paul during the past year, she writes, "I caught myself wishing Paul were with me" (159). As she stands alone on the prairie, lost and isolated, the wind becomes for her a metaphor for the "winds and tides of life" which have passed around her leaving her unfulfilled: "And I think of Paul, and wonder might it have been different if we had known each other earlier. Then the currents might have taken and fulfilled me. I might not still be nailed by them against a heedless wall" (160). Taking the metaphor further, the "heedless wall" to which she is nailed becomes Philip; "heedless" indicates his lack of love for her; "a wall" his staunch, enduring protectiveness notwithstanding her possessiveness; "nailed," their irrevocable union in marriage. This moment shortly before leaving Horizon is the closest Mrs. Bentley comes to admitting even to herself her affection for Paul which, nevertheless, has been lurking beneath the surface; in her journal from time to time she has mentioned how relaxed and comfortable they are together or remarked on their ability to be silent yet at ease with one another. The moment when Mrs. Bentley wonders whether life might have been different had she met Paul early is particularly significant since it occurs after the Bentleys appear to have resolved the major problems of their marriage. They have agreed to adopt Judith's baby, money from their various parishes is coming in regularly, and their plans to leave the town are almost complete.

Paul precipitates Mrs. Bentley's admission to Philip that she knows he is the father of Judith's child. This is his final contribution to the Bentley fortunes. While Philip is absent Mrs. Bentley becomes so frightened by a violent windstorm that she begs Paul to stay with her. The scene is fraught with tension: she herself admits that it was unfair to ask him to remain with her, "understanding things now as I did." As usual, she concludes the evening by playing the piano for Paul: "But I could feel him watching me all the time, and for escape at last I stopped suddenly and said, 'I think I hear the baby.' I brought him out of the bedroom to show Paul, but instead of looking at him Paul kept his eyes fixed on me. And the expression in his eyes was so wondering and incredulous that I realized he knew what all along I was certain I was keeping secret" (162). The culmination of this scene is Philip's arrival as Paul and Mrs. Bentley are in the bedroom with the baby. When Philip refuses to listen to her explanation, she angrily blurts out her knowledge that the baby is his. This revelation destroys a major barrier between the Bentleys and, therefore, is one of the most optimistic incidents in the novel; it allows the Bentleys to begin their new life more honestly.

Mrs. Bentley's relationship with Paul counterpoints that of Philip with Judith. Whereas she hints that perhaps if she had met Paul

earlier she might have been more fulfilled, the reader wonders
whether Judith might not have been a better mate for Philip. It is
ironic that both these affairs—Judith and Philip, Mrs. Bentley and
Paul—act as catalysts stimulating the Bentleys to actions which ultimately free them to start again together, while Paul remains in the
small town in which he will aways be an outsider and Judith's
dreams end in death.

Paul functions to some extent as a spokesman for the author. He
often says what the author wishes to be said but Mrs. Bentley cannot say. In contrast to the Bentleys, he is not a hypocrite. He takes
care to point out to them, for example, that although he attends the
mission service regularly with them he is a rationalist. His honesty
of expression frequently causes consternation among the townspeople. When he insists to the school children, for example, that
"belly" is a perfectly good word, " 'Cows may have them,' says
Mrs. Wenderby' 'and you, Mr. Kirby, but not my daughter Isobel
or I' " (70). As a teacher, Paul is the town intellectual; he quotes
mythology to link Philip, and his youthful sacrifices to buy books,
with Odin, Ulysses, and Faust; he lectures Mrs. Bentley on the
geological formation of the hills and their hundred-million-year-old
past, and quotes Nietzsche's *Thus Spoke Zarathustra* to warn her
against responding in kind to the sharp-tongued townspeople:
"Better to run off to the wilderness where there's a strong clean
wind blowing," says Paul. "It isn't man's lot to be a fly-flap" (133).[4]
Paul, a farm boy, provides, along with the Partridge Hill farmers, a
contrast to the townspeople in openness, honesty, and reliability.

VII   *The Artist*

It has been suggested that this novel is a *Kunstlerroman*,[5] but
rather than the story of a young artist, it is the story of a man of
thirty-five who has not succeeded in achieving his youthful ambition. Philip's wish to be a painter is tied to his wish to emulate his
father. His youthful interest in painting reflected his search for a
father, his search for roots, and search for a god. The urge to create
brought Philip to the ministry which seemed a door to the outside
world where he could find fulfillment. University experience did
not prove to be the liberating force he had anticipated; the artistic
life as he saw it in the college town proved limited and disappointing, but Philip continued to hope for success in a broader world
beyond. Marriage postponed this possibility.

Shut in his study, Philip goes on with his sketching. Whether he has the talent his wife sees in him is never made clear. Within the novel his search for artistic expression is paradigmatic of his search for self-liberation and self-expression. Although he assures his wife that it is not she who is keeping him a small-town preacher, but "the limitations of his hand and eye" (33), Mrs. Bentley is uncertain, and in fact some months later seems quite convinced of the contrary, that he is a genuine artist whose lack of development is her responsibility. Philip's art, however, while still linked with his earlier search for roots and identity, has become by this time a means of escaping the possessiveness of his wife as well, an excuse to shut the door of his study, shutting her out of a part of his life.

Because of the limited point of view, that of the diarist, Mrs. Bentley, and Philip's own reticence, his paintings, which project his feelings, become the major device whereby he is revealed to the reader. By reading carefully the descriptions of his sketches and paintings, the reader can perceive what is going on inside Philip to a greater extent than his wife does. The first day in Horizon, while they are unpacking, Mrs. Bentley turns over the sheet of paper on which Philip is writing his first sermon for the town and finds that "sure enough on the back of it there was a little Main Street sketched. It's like all the rest, a single row of smug, false-fronted stores, a loiterer or two, in the distance the prairie again. And like all the rest there's something about it that hurts. False fronts ought to be laughed at, never understood or pitied. They're such outlandish things, the front of a store built up to look like a second storey. They ought always to be seen that way, pretentious, ridiculous, never as Philip sees them, stricken with a look of self-awareness and futility" (4). These false fronts "stricken with a look of self-awareness and futility," may be seen as projections of Philip's own hypocrisy, his awareness of it, and his sense of futility. The sermon he is writing, based on the text *As For Me and My House We Will Serve the Lord*, declares what Philip, supposedly, stands for. As Mrs. Bentley says: "Sermon and drawing together, they're a kind of symbol, a summing up. The small-town preacher and the artist—what he is and what he nearly was—the failure, the compromise, the going-on—it's all there—the discrepancy between the man and the little niche that holds him" (4). Equally important, however, is the fact that the sermon appears on the front of the page, whereas the expression of Philip's true view of himself and of the little town is hidden on the back, much as his outward role as minister masks his real interest, that which he believes to be his true vocation, art.

Another sketch by Philip a week later can be seen to reveal his sense of the hopelessness of his own situation and his desire to escape from it:

. . . he's been drawing again. A cold, hopeless little thing—just the night as he left it at the front door. The solitary street lamp, pitted feebly and uselessly against the overhanging darkness. A little false-fronted store, still and blank and white—another—another—in retreating, steplike sequence—a stairway into the night. The insolent patch of the store is unabashed by the loom of darkness over it. The dark windows are like sockets of unlidded eyes, letting more of the night gape through. Farther on is a single figure, bent low, hurrying, almost away. One second more and the little street will be deserted. (16 - 17)

Here the reader can see that the false-fronted stores "in steplike sequence" indicate the endless succession of small prairie towns which have been Philip's past and which stretch in endless progression into the future, "a stairway into the night." The figure hurrying away can be interpreted as a reflection of Philip's desire to escape from this endless repetition of small towns. Sketches such as these contribute to Ross's portrayal of Philip—the hopelessness, frustration, and despair of his marriage and of his situation as a minister in this town.

Since his art is an unconscious projection of his feelings, the changes in Philip's art reveal the changes occurring within him. The first change in his painting takes place at the ranch. Instead of small-town Main Streets with their false-fronts and mean-eyed congregations, Philip paints hills and rivers. Philip's drawing of Laura's buckskin stallion indicates his understanding of this former rodeo star, whose dilemma is much like his own. She, too, is locked into a restrictive life and she, in her turn, understands the virile man compressed into a small town preacher who draws "little pictures." Laura's "I wish I had the handling of him for a day or two" (102), suggests she could cope with Philip better than his wife. Despite an angry flare-up with Laura, Philip is sufficiently stirred by her to spend his last two days at the ranch on his painting for her. To his wife's surprise, "for once, he had stooped to copy" (104); what Mrs. Bentley fails to note is that in making the painting as a gift, he has for once disregarded his own self-expression to please someone else.

To his wife's further surprise he is pleased with the approval with which others greet the painting. She should not be surprised, however, because earlier Philip had shown his pleasure at Paul's admiration of a painting. As Mrs. Bentley describes that incident: "He did a little prairie scene in oils this afternoon—on cardboard, because he wants to save the canvases till he's found himself in paints again—and when I called Paul in after school to look at it he screwed his face up hard to keep me from suspecting he was pleased. He was pleased even more though when Paul stood quite still in front of it a minute; so pleased that relaxing a little he asked him to stay for supper with us, and was nicer to him than he's ever been" (91). These comments also hint at the possibility that Mrs. Bentley's understanding of her husband is not as complete as she believes.

The most dramatic change in Philip's drawing is seen, however, only after his affair with Judith: "It's a string of galloping broncos, done with such a light, deft touch that you can feel space and air and freedom, and hear the ring of their hooves" (128). His creative impulse, stirred by his communion with nature at the ranch, is to an even greater extent given new life by love shared with a woman who loves and appreciates him. Surely, too, Philip's earlier preoccupation with sketching Judith was an indication of his attraction to her: "It's Judith tonight he's drawing. Or rather, trying to draw, for the strange swift whiteness of her face eludes him. The floor is littered with torn-up, crumpled sketches. He's out of himself, wrestling. There's a formidable wrinkle across his forehead, and in his eyes tense moments of immobile glare" (24). In a revealing scene not long afterwards, Mrs. Bentley shows Judith the drawings of her. In this instance, Philip is so pleased with Judith's admiration that he shows her other drawings, and finally, as she watches, makes another of her and one of himself, and gives both to Judith to take home. This behavior stands in contrast to his reaction to his wife's presence in his study. He cannot draw when she is present. At the lowest point in the Bentley marriage, when Philip is convinced of his wife's love for Paul and when Judith has returned home in disgrace to have her baby, Philip's painting reflects the hopelessness of the situation. He paints two horses frozen upright against a fence. They had died too exhausted to turn and face the wind. As Mrs. Bentley describes the painting, "a good job, if it's good in a picture to make you feel terror and pity and desolation" (153). These emotions, "terror and pity and desolation" can be seen to express the Bentleys' situation: their despair, their inability to turn and face the wind, which in this context symbolizes life itself.

As his artist's name indicates, the wolfhound El Greco is a paradigm for Philip. Philip's remark about the wolfhound could well apply to himself: "Town's no place for him, making a fool of himself. . . ." (118). Paul, too, agrees that El Greco should be out in the country running down coyotes: "It really isn't right, such a fine dog going to waste, playing in the street and making a fool of himself. . . . He's ashamed inside—knows this isn't where he ought to be" (137). Ironically, Mrs. Bentley fails to see the parallel with their situation in Horizon. As Philip hesitates to make a move, trying by writing religious articles to further his career in the ministry rather than daring to make the break, so too is El Greco, although he longs for the hunter's life, afraid to leave. As Paul says, when El Greco wanders out one evening, he is "stopped now on the edge of town, afraid to go any farther. You don't need to worry. He'll be back for his blankets and bread,and milk" (137). El Greco finally dies because he was never given the opportunity to live the life for which he was destined. He goes too far afield one night and, unprepared for coyotes, is killed by them. The attitude of the Bentleys to El Greco, when seen as a reflection of their own fear to face life, is fraught with irony:

> He was a wolfhound; we should have let him live like one. Paul kept telling us, but we argued he was better this way than like the poor, clapsided brutes that come to town sometimes with the farmers from the hills. Paul explained that they keep them hungry so they'll be keen for hunting, that in a hound's life bread and milk and safety can never make up for the excitement of a single kill, but Philip and I, of course, decided we knew better. (149)

When Philip breaks away from the town, he will have an opportunity for the life which he believes he was intended to have. Whether it is too late for him, as for El Greco, remains to be seen. For whether Philip will ever succeed as an artist is not resolved in the novel. He will, at least, have his opportunity in a different milieu, free of the guilt involved in preaching a religion he does not believe, and with a son to give his life the incentive it has lacked.

VIII   *The Bentley Marriage*

Mrs. Bentley is the most ambiguous figure in the novel. Her journal entries reveal as much about her as about her husband who is the center of her attention. But they must be read carefully, for, as we have seen, their significance is often hidden in metaphor which is usually not appreciated even by the writer herself. Because of

Mrs. Bentley's centrality, the story of the marriage takes precedence over the story of the artist.

Mrs. Bentley's first entry in her diary provides an indication of her attitude to her husband:

> He looks old and worn-out tonight; and as I stood over him a little while ago his face brought home to me how he shrinks from another town, how tired he is, and heartsick of it all. I ran my fingers through his hair, then stooped and kissed him. Lightly, for that is of all things what I mustn't do, let him ever suspect me of being sorry. He's a very adult, self-sufficient man, who can't bear to be fussed or worried over; and sometimes, broodless old woman that I am, I get impatient being just his wife, and start in trying to mother him too. (4)

Aware of Philip's resentment of his mother, "towards even her memory he remained implacable" (30), Mrs. Bentley's maternal behavior is unlikely to draw Philip closer. The tension of their relationship is indicated by her need to fight against her instinct to give him a simple gesture of affection and to consciously hide her feelings of sympathy, "for that is of all things what I musn't do, let him ever suspect me of being sorry."

Connected with Mrs. Bentley's mothering tendencies is her tendency to belittle Philip's manual skill. "I could use the pliers and hammer twice as well myself, with none of his mutterings or smashed-up fingers either," she says. She claims that it is because of the town's expectations that she "let him be the man about the house, and sat on a trunk among the litter serenely making curtains over. . . ." Although Mrs. Bentley insists that this domestic scene is intended to impress Horizon with their fulfillment of expected roles, the actual result is that when visitors arrive, "Philip, his nerves all ragged, and a smear of soot across his face, didn't make a particularly good impression." One wonders then at the point of the pretence. This first day and first entry suggest that hypocrisy has become a way of life with the Bentleys.

Some months later, Mrs. Bentley is even more aggravating as she harps at Philip to put up the heater, "Why can't you take hold and do things like other men?" (133). Her comments about her husband's uselessness are contradicted by his actions at a Main Street fire; here he takes the lead, efficiently directing operations so that, to the town's admiration, he brings the fire under control. The intimation is that Philip can act more effectively than his wife wants to admit. She encourages the portrait of his ineffectuality and her own capability.

The Bentleys' contrasting attitude to hypocrisy is demonstrated by Mrs. Bentley's anecdote about Philip's pipe. She recalls that in early years he smoked in secret, hiding his pipe and ordering tobacco in an unmarked wrapper. When he angrily threw away his pipe, she unperceptively construed his behavior as a temporary loss of patience with the involved procedure. Because she did not share his guilt at the pretence involved, she failed to understand that he was rejecting his own hypocritical behavior. On the contrary, she recalls nostalgically the sense of sharing which their connivance in his smoking gave her: "It was easier when Philip smoked. The silences were less strained, the study door between us less implacable. The pipe belonged to both of us. We were partners in conspiracy" (14). For Philip such pretence is now unbearable. He may be trapped in his role as a minister, but he will no longer add to the hypocrisy of his situation in these trivial ways.

Moving to a new town causes Mrs. Bentley to look about her, to consider her future and also her past. How did they get here? Where are they going? She assesses the present and sees the gulf between herself and her husband widening. She considers the past and admits that she had manipulated Philip into marriage:

Had I not met him then he might have got away as he planned, eventually realized his ambitions.

For a long time he held aloof. At heart, I think, he was distrustful not only of me but all my kind. It was friendship he wanted, someone to realize in flesh and blood the hero-worship that he had clung to all through his hard adolescence. He would just half-yield himself to me, then stand detached, self-sufficient. It was as if this impulse to seek me out made him feel guilty, as if he felt he were being false to himself. Perhaps, too, he knew instinctively that as a woman I would make claims upon him, and that as an artist he needed above all things to be free.

I was patient. I tried hard. Now sometimes I feel it a kind of triumph, the way I won my place in his life despite him; but other times I see his eyes frustrated, slipping past me, a spent, disillusioned stillness in them, and I'm not so sure. It's hard to feel yourself a hindrance, to stand back watching a whole life go to waste. (33)

Mrs. Bentley's ambivalence concerning her action is apparent. Although triumphant at having "won my place in his life despite him," seeing his frustration and disappointment, she admits to herself, "I'm not so sure." Her journal becomes a means for her to explore her dilemma, to try to discover what is happening to their lives and their marriage.

Music is the means whereby Mrs. Bentley first met Philip. Later her playing of a Liszt rhapsody lured him into proposing to her. As a matter of fact, music makes Mrs. Bentley, despite her protestations of her dowdy nondescript appearance, into an amalgam of Pied Piper and Circe. Her piano playing attracts young and old of both sexes. Passersby stop at the door to listen; the doctor's wife walks in unannounced exclaiming, "That's why I dropped in on you, my dear. I heard your piano up on Main Street—young, sparkling, jubilant—" (21); even the Ladies Aid invites her to play. The first time she meets Paul and Judith, they are impressed with her organ music, and both visit the Bentleys to listen to her at the piano. Aware of her talent, she uses it deliberately to attract others. Having first won Philip with a rhapsody, she attempts to win him back with the same piece, but ironically it captivates Paul instead. She successfully lures Steve away from Philip with the piano. With music reduced to such ends, small wonder that the sound of the piano sets Philip pacing.

A consideration of these attitudes of Mrs. Bentley helps us see why the Bentley marriage is in a precarious state on their arrival in Horizon. Mrs. Bentley's maternalism includes an overmotherly solicitude and a tendency to see her husband as childishly inept. The Bentleys' views towards the hypocritical situation in which they live are opposed; she accepts and contributes to it, even rejoicing in their joint efforts to deceive the town; while he rejects any additional pretence, finding himself increasingly distraught at the hypocrisy required by his vocation. Their marriage, which is largely responsible for Philip's present dilemma, has been, as Mrs. Bentley admits, her own doing.

Primarily through three events of the year in Horizon—the adoption of Steve, the holiday at the ranch, and Judith's pregnancy—Mrs. Bentley comes to appreciate her claustrophobic possessiveness, to regret the pretence involved even in her relationship with her husband, and to take steps to escape from the small town. With Steve's arrival, she sees how eager and rejuvenated Philip appears, and finds herself alternating between pleasure and jealousy. As she tries to sort out her feelings, she is forced to admit "I'm not used to coming second in his life," and, "Of course I've been wrong. Sitting here quiet and tired now I understand things better. All these years I've been trying to possess

him, to absorb his life into mine, and not once has he ever yielded,"
and a few minutes later, "He was never really mine to lose to
anyone. These false-fronted little towns have been holding us
together, nothing else. It's no use a woman's thinking that if she
loves a man patiently and devotedly enough she can eventually
make him love her too. Philip married me because I made myself
important to him, consoled him when he was despondent, stroked
his vanity the right way. I meant well" (64). Trying to understand
her own emotions and motives, she writes, "It's the reason perhaps
I still care so much, the way he's never let me possess him, always
held himself withdrawn. For love, they say, won't survive possession. After a year or two it changes, cools, emerges from its
blindness, at best becomes affection and regard. And mine hasn't"
(65).

Mrs. Bentley's awareness of her responsibility for the failure of
their marriage comes to a head at the ranch. Toward the end of
their holiday as she takes stock of herself she admits that she has
"contrived" to fool herself:

> It seems that tonight for the first time in my life I'm really mature. Other
> times, even when trying to be honest with myself, I've always contrived to
> think that at least we had each other, that what was between us was strong
> and genuine enough to compensate for all the rest. But tonight I'm doubt-
> ful. All I see is the futility of it. It destroyed him; it leaves me alone outside
> his study door. I'm not bitter, just tired, whipped. I see things clearly. The
> next town—the next and the next. There doesn't seem much meaning to
> our going on. (103)

By closing the study door, she now sees, Philip is shutting her out
psychologically and spiritually as well as physically. It is his way of
fighting her possessiveness. His silence and withdrawal add to the
tension of their relationship as they sit tautly aware of each other
through the closed study door. Whether she sees things as clearly as
she believes at this time is debatable. However, on their return to
Horizon, Mrs. Bentley acknowledges her responsibility for Philip
still being in the Church: "For these last twelve years I've kept him
in the Church—no one else. The least I can do now is help get him
out again" (107). Determined to get Philip out of the ministry, she
now conceives the idea of a book and music store in the city.

Mrs. Bentley's failure of creativity is seen not only in her inability
to produce a child, but in her garden which shrivels and dries up in
the summer drought, and her flowers that freeze in the winter. To

the reader, Mrs. Bentley's dried up garden is a reflection of the couple's emotional aridity and disappointed hopes, the spiritual, cultural, and emotional barrenness of their lives.

Judith gives the final impetus to the Bentleys. When Mrs. Bentley discovers Philip's affair with Judith, she becomes even more determined to get her husband out of the ministry and out of Horizon. The decision to adopt Judith's baby gives Philip the impetus to leave the ministry and the hypocrisy associated with it.

As they leave Horizon, the Bentleys are optimistic about the future. Philip is freed from the guilt of preaching a faith he does not believe. He has a son. Now he may be able to find release for his creativity. Mrs. Bentley has gained in self-knowledge: she has recognized her possessiveness and the effect it has had on their marriage. Yet the situation, although hopeful, remains ambiguous. Mrs. Bentley is partly, but not entirely, aware of her own role in the threatened breakdown of their marriage. She realizes her tendency to interfere. On the other hand, she continues to view herself as "In workaday matters . . . so much more practical and capable than he is," and when she adds to this comment, "in a month or two I'd be one of those domineering females that men abominate" (160), it is obvious that she still does not appreciate how domineering she actually has been, or comprehend Philip's intense resentment of her domination. Mrs. Bentley's final words in the novel contribute to the ambiguous note on which it ends; her indication that her attitude toward both of the two Philips (her husband and the baby) will be the same, is one of the double-edged remarks of the novel:[6] indicating an equal love is good; but also suggesting a mothering attitude—knowing her husband's rejection of mothering—is not wise. But the new locale and new vocation, and the opportunities these provide for a different perspective, give reason to view the conclusion of the novel with some hope.

Much as the narrative acts in two directions, outwardly to reveal Philip and inwardly to reveal the writer of the journal, so is the movement in the novel in two different directions. The external action of adopting the baby and moving out of Horizon parallels the internal change whereby Mrs. Bentley grows in self-knowledge, so that the possibility of better understanding and more communication in the future remains open.

The ambiguity of Mrs. Bentley's character is a major aspect of this novel's fascination. On a first reading of *As For Me and My House*, the reader may tend to be sympathetic with her situation, admire her intelligence, her fortitude, and her determination to save her husband and herself from an unending future of Horizons. However, when one reads not only what Mrs. Bentley is reporting but what the imagery and action are revealing, the obverse of Mrs. Bentley's qualities becomes apparent. Her love for her husband is too possessive, her determination too manipulative, her attitude to the town too hypocritical, and her assessment of others and of what is happening frequently incorrect.

The confessional mode allows us to view the Bentley marriage from within the mind of one of the partners. Mrs. Bentley's attempts to understand what is happening to her marriage eventually leads her to some understanding of what is happening to herself. Through the incidents she selects as sufficiently meaningful to be reported and commented upon in her journal, the reader participates in her emotional reactions to her husband and to the community. She unwittingly reveals more of herself than she realizes through her description of the town with its inhabitants, and of the prairie landscape with its wind, rain, and drought. In fact, both the Bentleys are revealed most clearly by their projections of themselves; the taciturn Philip speaks through his paintings, his wife through her perception of the town and landscape.

The style of the novel, which is compressed, metaphorical, and indirect, is largely responsible for its density and complexity. At the same time, *As For Me and My House* remains one of Canada's most effective regional novels. It fulfills the promise of Ross's early prairie stories in which inner tension and conflict were mirrored in the landscape.

CHAPTER 4

The Well

IN *The Well* Ross focuses on a central character who moves from an urban to a rural environment, and on the internal transformation which the new environment engenders. While there are a number of echoes of earlier works, the texture of this novel is thinner. Once again the setting is rural Saskatchewan, nature plays a central role, and entrapment is a major theme.

Twenty-year-old Chris Rowe, having shot a man in an abortive robbery, is fleeing from Montreal police. It remains uncertain throughout the novel whether the injured man, Baxter, dies later, but the implication is that he does not. When Chris jumps off a freight train at the small prairie town of Campkin he intends only to cadge a meal and continue West. But he meets an elderly farmer, Larson, who buys him a meal and offers him a job. This strikes Chris as an opportunity to hide out and at the same time earn the money to further continue his flight.

The plot revolves around Chris's relationship with Larson and with Larson's young wife, Sylvia, and the gradual change in Chris's attitude brought about by his growing attachment to the land and the farm animals, to a mode of life which is the complete antithesis of his former one as member of a tough city neighborhood gang. Nature becomes a redemptive force for Chris.

I *Significance of the Past*

The time span of the novel is seven or eight weeks of late summer, from the beginning of harvest to a week or so later. Through various techniques of retrospective narration, Ross interweaves the past with the present. Thus the reader becomes aware of previous experiences which have helped mold the three central characters: Chris, Larson, and Sylvia. Chris is the center of intelligence through whom events and characters are perceived. He is continually looking back to incidents and individuals of his childhood and youth, thus revealing the forces which have contributed to his formation as an arrogant, insecure, young criminal.

Early pages of the novel disclose that as a small child Chris had lived with his mother in a single room. Later, when she took one lover after another, the young boy became jealous and insecure. None of these temporary intruders on family life accepted him as a son. Feeling very much alone, he learned early in life that he could buy friends among the boys on the street with money extorted from his mother who sought to ease her feelings of guilt about her own way of life. With the Boyle Street gang Chris became involved in petty crime: robbery of neighborhood stores, back alley muggings, and, finally, the incident in which he, having been recognized by his would-be robbery victim, in a panic shot him. Ross hints at a potentially gentle, sensitive nature in Chris that has never had an opportunity to develop, and suggests that Chris is in many ways the victim of circumstances. An early indication of Chris's possible redemption is the name Mackenzie which he takes to hide his identity. Mackenzie was a teacher who had tried to persuade him to leave the Boyle Street gang and take his studies seriously.

Larson, too, harkens back to the past. He had lost his first wife, Cora, ten years earlier. Their only son, who also was named Chris, was killed a short time later. Larson is haunted by memories of both. His three sections of farmland, new Cadillac, and young wife are tokens of his present success. But because he has no one with whom to share them, they have no meaning. He attempts to preserve the past by fencing in his old house, sod barn, and well, even planning to repaint the dilapidated old house. The well, in particular, which Larson and Cora had dug the summer after their wedding, is a symbol of his happiest years. In many ways Larson attempts to bring back this past. He had shot his son's horse which had been responsible for the boy's death, but since then has always kept a horse with similar markings which he calls by the same name, Minnie. He keeps a dog resembling his son's former dog. To achieve some satisfaction from his successful farm, he imagines the boy returning each year to be shown changes and improvements. Larson lives in a world of illusion because present reality, despite his obvious material success, is empty for him. Five years previously he had married in an attempt to find satisfaction in the present moment; but the marriage is a failure and Larson must continue to cling to his illusory world.

II *Ambivalence and Change*

Ross effectively shows Chris's changing attitude to the prairie. As he drives with Larson the first time from the town into the countryside, the immensity of the prairie frightens him: "The foreground at least was to human scale, but his imagination, fixed in its alley-doorway patterns, shrank from the stark, sky-and-earth immensity. It seemed desert-like and sinister." [1] As Larson stops on the side of the road to point out his farm, Chris demonstrates the reaction of the city dweller to this alien world:

A big white house, a big red barn, a gleaming, silvery silo; but Chris's eyes slipped past them, unarrested. From where they stood the prairie fell in easy, wrinkled undulations half-way to the horizon, spread out a few miles, flat as the surface of a lake, and then, gathering the last faint momentum of its descent, slid smoothly to a standstill like a spent toboggan against a range of stubby sand-hills. He still felt oppressed, uneasy. It was his first contact with the open country; the bare expanse spread out before him now seemed gaping, mutilated, as if a giant shovel had sheared away something essential, like features from a face. He would never fit in, never survive. The feeling of exposure and inadequacy was so strong that it cost him an effort not to retreat to the truck and slam the door. He wanted to shout to Larson to take him back to town. (13)

But when Chris arrives at the farm his reaction to his small bedroom is the antithesis of his reaction to the prairie. "In its effect on him the close, cupboard-like room was an inversion of the open prairie. Driving along in the truck he had felt exposed, conspicuous. Here he was trapped, a prisoner" (22). These two contrasting reactions mirror the dilemma in which he finds himself as a fugitive. He must either continue to flee, feeling always threatened and exposed, as he does on the prairie; or he must surrender, and accept imprisonment in a cell which would be much like the "close, cupboard-like room" on the farm. Ross's technique here is similar to that employed in *As For Me and My House*. Chris's impression of the prairie as "desert-like and sinister" and of the room as "close, cupboard-like" making him feel "trapped, a prisoner" are, like Mrs. Bentley's impressionistic view of town and prairie, projections of his own interior fears onto his external surroundings.

In contrast to his fear of both the open prairie and the enclosed room, Chris's first response to the barn is "It's so still—makes you feel sort of safe and shut away" (38). It is here that Chris achieves his first sense of belonging. Through the two old workhorses, Ned and Fanny, who are linked to the years of struggle building this farm, Chris begins to understand and respect the weak and the old, and those who work—all of whom he had previously derided as "fools" or "suckers." For Fanny who, after sixteen colts and twenty-five years behind a plow, is "grateful for her oats and a friendly word," Chris feels respect "such as he had never felt for a woman" (56). With the black stallion, North, he feels an immediate kinship. Like Chris, North has vanity, high spirits, and a need to show off; like Chris he is "always figuring out how much he can get away with" (45). With the young sorrel, Minnie, Chris finds solace when frightened or lonely. As he buries his face in her shoulder Chris is behaving much as earlier Ross protagonists whose horses provided an outlet for emotional expression. Chris finds trust and friendship with the animals he could never find with the Boyle Street gang. The horses give him a sense of being needed. With them he need fear no betrayal; he needs no façade. Chris responds to them as he never has to people—with gentleness, respect, trust, and friendship. The changes initiated by these experiences begin to effect other areas of his life, as his attitude to the prairie indicates: "The first few days the prairie had seemed aloof and desert-like; now he felt himself part of it, at home. Each time he turned reluctantly, wishing he could ride all day" (52).

The horse is a recurrent image in Ross's works. This is to be expected as most of his fiction is set in a time when the horse was indispensable to the prairie farmer. In Ross, the horse takes on varying roles. For his children it is linked to the imaginative life—Peter Parker's colt becomes his Pegasus, and Jenny's old roan, Billie, is transformed into a young, fleet-footed circus horse. For the adolescent Peter McAlpine, the young mare, Isabel, associated with his initiation into manhood, has qualities linking her with sexuality and imagination. To the adult Peter in *Whir of Gold*, Isabel functions as a link with his past and a continuing reminder of his own talent and superiority.

For Ross's farmers the horse is a companion, and sometimes a reliable and accepting surrogate for a dissatisfied wife; Paul leaves his frightened and rebellious wife alone in the house while he seeks comfort and assurance from his mare, Bess, in the barn; John, refusing to show emotion before his wife when hail destroys his crop, sobs alone into the neck of his horse. In "The Runaway" the Black Diamond horses are a symbol of prestige, both for their breeder, Luke Taylor, and for the farmer who is duped into buying them.

Demonstration of the skills of horsemanship and of mastery of the animal are associated with masculinity. Not long after they meet, Paul Kirby rides his horse to the Bentley house to show off his riding skills to Mrs. Bentley; young Peter McAlpine proves his daring to his schoolmate, Millie, by riding Isabel. In most instances, the horse which is linked with sexuality is a young mare. Chris Rowe, however, demonstrates his virility by handling the stallion, North. His relationship with the stallion is closer to D. H. Lawrence's use of the horse as symbol of masculine potency.

In the maturing of Chris, the horses play a variety of roles. As he adapts to farm life Chris begins to develop as an independent human being: "For on Boyle Street even his thoughts had never been quite his own. There was always the need to think and do according to the expectations of the gang. Because he existed only in the reflections they gave back, he was at their mercy, even while he went among them, assured and slickly superior. But here he could relax, slip a little, and it concerned no one but himself. No mirrors, no reflections—it was almost freedom" (56 - 57). The mirror image indicates how false his previous way of life had been. He had been living a role with no real existence beyond others' views of him. Now for the first time, no longer living and acting only in response to the gang, he begins to feel free. Yet Chris vacillates between his old way of life and this new one, his old desire for the easy life, resentment of discipline, need to show off, and the new and surprising satisfaction to be found in work, closeness to nature, trust in and affection for the farm animals. Although interaction with the natural world—landscape, animals, and the simple activities of farm life—gradually alters Chris's sense of values, the change is marked by abrupt swings and bursts of anger.

III   *Larson, Chris and Sylvia*

Larson's liking for him also adds to Chris's growing sense of self-worth. As he begins to trust the old farmer, Chris's gentle nature begins to show through his tough exterior. From his first meeting with Chris, Larson addresses him as "son," for his name and age allow him to see in Chris his own son, had he lived. It is soon evident that Larson hopes to find a surrogate son in Chris, to find in this present reality a replacement for his own illusory world. Larson, though, is irascible and unpredictable; he vacillates in his behavior to Chris, struggles to assess Chris's worthiness to be accepted as a son and also to transfer his own allegiance from the past to the present—from the fantasy pretence of a dead son's return to the possibility of finding a genuine son in this young stranger. His vacillation parallels Chris's own ambivalence.

The major complicating factor in their relationship is Sylvia. Sylvia is a big, attractive, blonde woman, thirty years younger than Larson, who married him to escape her dreary waitressing job. Now, after five years in a loveless union, she finds herself just as trapped as she had been previously; she has escaped the past into an equally disagreeable present. That Larson views her as another possession, his words, "I got her in Regina," obviously indicate. Their marriage was strictly a business arrangement. He has agreed to give her a sum of money each year. In return she fulfills her various functions as his wife. For Larson an attractive young wife is a further reminder, like his new Cadillac, that he is a success. It is hardly surprising that the relationship is such a disappointment to both partners.

Sylvia, like Larson, hopes to solve her problems through Chris. She recognizes an affinity with the tough, arrogant, goodlooking young man, for both are products of a rugged, urban experience. His arrival reinforces her determination to free herself of Larson. By seducing Chris she hopes to win his affection and implicate him in the murder of her husband. The struggle for Chris between Larson and Sylvia is the external expression of Chris's internal struggle.

Sylvia and Chris understand each other from their first meeting. Both are accustomed to using other people. Both are trying to escape—Chris from the past, including his responsibility for injuring and possibly killing someone, Sylvia from the present—Larson. Sylvia's objective is money and the freedom to enjoy it. This was once Chris's objective, too, until his experiences on the farm began to show him the possibility of a different way of life with a different set of values. Chris's wavering between Sylvia and Larson is analogous to his fluctuations between his former Boyle Street mode of life and the new, more honest values of rural life. There is no love in the relationship between Chris and Sylvia, but only the wish of each to overpower and use the other.

IV   *The Oedipal Situation*

In many ways Sylvia is a mother-figure. She is older than Chris who sees her as stronger than he is. In their lovemaking Sylvia takes the initiative while Chris is passive and accepting: "Her hair fell

round his face and throat; he liked that. It tingled his skin, enclosed
him so that he could open his eyes without her knowing, without
committing himself to response or initiative. Her hands and lips
moved with gentle insistence, caressing, rousing, exploring, and as
the rich, big-breasted warmth of her body enveloped him he felt
small and childlike again, infinitely at peace" (127). The child-
mother relationship is further indicated when Chris discovers that
the old mare, Fanny, is about to give birth: "He stood still a moment, worried and helpless, not knowing what to do, then like a
child wheeled away and ran to the house to tell Sylvia" (207).

The traditional romantic triangle of husband-wife-lover develops into a symbolically oedipal one of son- father-figure- mother-
figure. The death of the father-figure, Larson, is indirectly
precipitated by the return of the son who, although he does not actually kill this father, does for a time, contemplate it, and is implicated when he helps to get rid of the body and evidence of the
crime. The oedipal situation is suggested also by the revelation of
Chris's childhood relationship with his mother when they lived
together in one room: "There had been trust, of course, in the
beginning. Just the two of them: a room with a cretonne curtain up
a splintery stair, canned soup heated on a gas ring in the hall, stale
cakes sometimes that she smuggled home to him from the bakery.
But the betrayal, when it came, made suspect even the memories of
his happy times. He looked back through the hurt as through a
cracked lens, and saw everything askew and darkened" (54). The
"betrayal" referred to is the taking of a lover by his mother. After
that time, Chris found his approval and satisfaction on the street
where money, combined with his good looks, bought him acceptance and power.

Chris's contempt for women, his closeness to the Boyle Street
gang, and especially his affection for Rickie, the street leader,
suggest homosexual tendencies. On Boyle Street, women are to be
used, possessed as status symbols like the fast cars and apartments
and trips Chris wants. Trading on his good looks, Chris had learned
to pick up a woman at a bar and later at her apartment rob her of
jewelry or money. When Sylvia disdains him on their first meeting,
Chris vows "Bitch—before you're finished you'll be begging for it.
Crawling!" (21). Women are to be seduced as a proof to himself of
his own superiority. Significantly, inexperienced young Elsie
Grover, whose naivety and innocence attract Chris, is more appeal-
ing to him in the boyish garb of their first meeting than in her frilly

dress and attempted femininity at the Saturday night dance. He seduces her to reassert his masculine dominance. Because he is fatherless Chris needs the male support and masculine admiration lacking in his childhood. Through Rickie, the gang leader who returns to Boyle Street after serving a prison sentence, Chris is initiated into a life of more serious crime involving dope deliveries and contact with fences. Rickie gives Chris an expensive ring and a watch, picks up the check when they go out together, and takes him on trips—all rituals of a traditional courtship. As he flees from the Montreal police, Chris is fleeing to Rickie on the West coast. Indications of latent homosexuality in Chris's relationship with Rickie may be viewed as the result of arrested emotional development caused by the absence of a father figure in his childhood.

V   *The Climax*

At the funeral of Cora's nephew, also significantly named Chris, events transpire which propel Larson, Chris, and Sylvia into a melodramatic climax. Ross skillfully and unobtrusively builds the suspense of the climactic scene through rhythm, repetition, and short, sharp sentences.

When he [Chris] entered the kitchen Larson was washing his hands at the sink. The table was set, and Sylvia was moving back and forth from the stove to the pantry. Neither of them looked at him. When he had dried his hands, Larson sat down at the table with a livestock paper that had come in the mail. A pan of meat was frying on the stove, the kettle was singing, yet there seemed to be no progress in the preparation of the meal. Chris, too, washed and dried his hands; Sylvia was still moving in and out of the pantry. His nerves were already frayed and twitching. Now the silence began to wear on them. It was like a conspiracy. It gave him a feeling of helplessness and exclusion. Suddenly he wheeled on Larson; his voice shot up harsh and loud. "What about my pay? You've been to town and you say you've got it all figured out. What are you stalling for?" (230)

Sylvia forces the moment to its climax by revealing her affair with Chris and then urging Larson to report their suspicions of Chris's past. As Larson is about to do so, she thrusts a gun into Chris's hand. When Chris, instead of shooting, drops the gun, he realizes that by deliberately making this choice, by refusing to buy his own safety, as it would seem, at the price of murdering Larson, he has freed himself. "He was free—there was room for nothing else. He had been living under a spell—of what he was, always had been, always must be, a doom of Boyle Street cheapness and frustration—and now the spell was broken. He had not obeyed. Even with the gun in his hand, he had not done it" (236). This is the moment toward which the action of the novel has been moving, the moment when Chris must choose between the two alternatives presented to him here: Boyle Street and the prairie, Sylvia and Larson, a superficial existence through impressing others and a self-sufficient life of work on the farm.

The chief structural weakness of the novel is not that this scene is melodramatic but that the series of climaxes which follow become more than the reader can accept. After a struggle for the gun, Sylvia herself shoots Larson. In another struggle, Chris succeeds in locking her out of the house while a dying Larson signs a note accusing Sylvia, exonerating Chris and leaving him the farm. With Larson dead Sylvia, by sheer will power, persuades Chris that he is too deeply implicated to withdraw; he unwillingly helps her carry the body to the old well. Finally on their return to the farm Chris summons the strength to report the murder, Sylvia flees, and Chris accepts the future—which will include a jail term for shooting Baxter—but, also, following this punishment, ownership of the farm and possibly the love of Elsie Grover. In his seesaw struggle with Sylvia, Chris ultimately comes out the victor. But his greatest victory is his achievement of selfhood, as he frees himself from his past for the first time squarely to face his situation, rather than running away. Here on the prairie he has found himself.

VI Style

The main method of rhetorical control employed by Ross in this novel is the interweaving of internal thought with external reaction to reveal the effect of Chris's farm experiences on his emotional and psychic life. The narrator allows the reader to get inside Chris, whose thoughts and dreams, ambitions and fears, emotions and reactions become exposed. This narrative method combines present action and retrospective narration, with Chris as the center of intelligence. Recollections of his past experiences explain his personality and account for his present uneasiness and fearfulness. Along with his thoughts, Chris's confused, nightmarish, and threatening dreams heighten the sense of his present precarious and unsettled position. Larson's past is gradually unfolded through his conversations with Chris. His nostalgic recollections of past struggles serve both to reveal his early years, and to indicate his own erratic fluctuations from past to present, from illusion—centered on memories of his wife and son—to reality. Skillful handling of time shifts is essential to the psychological development of the characters, for the tensions within both Larson and Chris are revealed to be the result of the dichotomy between their past and their present.

A further aspect of Ross's handling of time is his method of highlighting a cluster of incidents within a short time span. For example, in the first five chapters of the novel time moves slowly as Chris becomes acquainted with Larson, Sylvia, and the farm animals. Then time is speeded up until two weeks later, when it is again slowed down to detail the events which occur during one weekend. Although most of the incidents are in themselves trivial, their cumulative effect is to show Chris's gradual change in response to everyday events of farm life, and the developing relationship between the three central characters.

Narrative method is on occasion less subtle than in the other novels. Sometimes Ross tells the reader what he has already successfully shown him. For example, the reader is aware of the struggle in Larson's mind before the narrator explains, "Chris was reality, the boy an illusion. Abandoning the one for the other wasn't easy; . . ." (96). Also Chris has been seen beginning to mature—before the reader is told, unnecessarily—"Belatedly, growth was setting in" (54).

The major symbol in this novel is the well, which to Larson symbolizes the happiness of his early struggling years with Cora. His care of the well, which is fenced in and covered to keep the water clean, underlines his determination to preserve this past. His return to the well with Chris indicates his desire to link Chris with this happier time, as he does even more directly in seeking to make Chris his lost son. It is fitting that, having clung so tenaciously to this symbol of past happiness, at his death Larson should return to it. The significance of the well recalls Ross's first story, "No Other Way," in which the old well became for Hatty Glenn the focal point for remembrance of happier though less prosperous days.[2] In "No Other Way" the well was also linked with death, as the setting for Hatty's contemplation of suicide. In both instances the association of the well with death is in itself ironic, since as a source of water it is traditionally linked with creativity and life.

The birth of the colt to old Fanny takes on symbolic significance.

In Larson's absence, Chris assists with the delivery, while Sylvia, to whom Chris runs for help, refuses to become involved. As he struggles with the mare, Chris becomes smeared with pieces of the birth membrane, a indication that for him, too, there is a birth—into this farming community and the new life which it has come to signify for him. At this moment the other Chris, Cora's nephew, dies. Now Chris Rowe, as the only one of his name remaining, is Larson's true heir. Immediately after this event he is put to the test, placed in a situation parallel to that in which earlier he had shot a man. Chris's strength in rejecting murder in this instance clearly indicates his transformation, his choice on the side of life. His choice was prefigured by his involvement with the birth of the colt. On the other hand, Sylvia's deliberate and calculated planning and carrying out of the murder are prefigured by her refusal to assist in the delivery of the colt, a deliberate rejection of life.

Structurally, the ending of the novel is weak. The result for the three central characters is credible; events have led inexorably to a climactic scene between them and to a test for Chris, who has been vacillating between his past life and his new life and must make a choice. But the extended melodramatic seesaw battle between Chris and Sylvia which follows is unsatisfactory in terms of the tensions of the novel. A further weakness is the lack of development of Chris's relationship with young Elsie Grover, the village girl who serves as a contrast to Sylvia. Elsie remains a shadowy figure, and Chris's belief, when he gives himself up, that she may wait for him for ten years lacks credibility. An added problem in the novel is the handling of dreams. Chris's nightmares are the source of Sylvia's knowledge of his past and of the crime from which he is fleeing. Ross requires the reader to believe that Sylvia, lurking at Chris's bedroom door, pieces together the facts of his past from his confused dreamings and mutterings.

The Well lacks the metaphoric language of *As For Me and My House* and *Whir of Gold*. When colorful metaphor is occasionally employed it seems inappropriate, too precious for the harshness of theme and action and the personality of the central character. For example, the indication of Larson's penury as he momentarily hesitates to offer Chris a new razor blade is described as "another gritty calculus of thrift in the duct of good will" (24), an original but somewhat ornate image in this context. When Chris stretches his hand out for the first time to one of the horses, the reader is told, "But Chris's hand came closer, trembling with the strain like a com-

pass needle, till at last it reached the stallion's nose" (41). Although
as a description of movement the image of the compass needle is ac-
curate, it conveys no deeper meaning and hence appears somewhat
contrived.

A more successful metaphor describes Chris's delight at his
friendly reception on his first visit to town: "He sensed approval,
too, and here, as in Boyle Street, it was spark and sustenance, what
he lived by. The needle under the skin of his vanity, the shot of
euphoria, the little glow of poise and confidence—it was a familiar
sensation, . . ." (60). This image is expansive and resonant. Chris's
need for approval is indeed like the addict's need for a drug. Like a
drug, approval gives him a momentary glow, a temporary feeling of
self-confidence. Because the effect is so fleeting he must be continually seeking further means of winning approval, just as the addict must continue taking drugs to renew his glow: "There was
always the need to think and do according to the expectations of the
gang. Because he existed only in the reflections they gave
back, . . ." (56). The shooting which has made him a fugitive was
itself the outcome of a life directed by the need to win approval on
Boyle Street.

VII   Themes

The major theme of the novel is the regeneration of a tough
young criminal, a loner who is completely alienated from society.
Chris's vacillation is credibly portrayed and his final acceptance of
the consequences of his earlier actions brings him, paradoxically, his
first real freedom. The theme of the alienated man is a common one
in twentieth-century literature, but achievement of happiness
through acceptance into a community provides a characteristically
Canadian solution.[3]

Second only to the exploration of the criminal mind and its
transformation is the theme of illusion versus reality. Both Chris
and Larson live in unreal worlds. Larson's dissatisfaction with reality is symbolized by his frequent trips to town to watch the freight
trains coming and going, and his dreaming of escaping one day
himself. Year after year he continues to depend on the illusion of his
dead son returning to give meaning to his life, to his work, and to
his success. Chris lives in the illusory world of Boyle Street admiration and the power and happiness money can buy. Larson achieves
the reality he seeks only at the moment of death: when Chris

refuses to shoot him, he has found his son and signifies this by willing the farm to him. Chris achieves his reality when he finally faces the future he fears, including imprisonment.

Through both Chris and Larson materialism is shown to be an illusory source of happiness. Chris's reliance on money is ironically counterpointed by Larson's situation. Although a wealthy man, Larson, lonely and unhappy, looks back to his early, struggling years as his happiest. Interwoven with the theme of the illusory happiness gained through money is the romantic theme of the regenerative effects of nature.

Thematically, the novel has much in common with earlier works. The significance of the horses in Chris's development recalls young Steve's horse in *As For Me and My House*, and the central role of the horse as an agent of initiation in "The Outlaw" and as a source of solace and support in "A Field of Wheat" and "The Lamp at Noon." As in *As For Me and My House* the longing for a son is central to this novel. And as in *As For Me and My House* Chris shares with Mrs. Bentley the feeling of exposure resulting from the immensity of the prairie. His fear of the "wet black void that lay beyond" signifies for him, as it did for Mrs. Bentley, a fear of the future, of the unknown, and suggests the lack of a spiritual or psychological base which would enable him to act decisively, to face the unknown and unpredictable future.

This novel is not as successful as Ross's earlier and later novels. The absence of humor is unusual for Ross. Despite its flaws, *The Well* remains an intricately devised study of a weak young man whose background has led him to a life of petty crime, but who gradually changes through the impact of the natural world and his relationship with a father-figure.

CHAPTER 5

Whir of Gold

WHIR of Gold did not appear until twelve years after *The
Well*. It was written during Ross's last years in Montreal and
refined after his retirement in Greece. With this novel Ross returns
to the richer texture and more metaphorical language of *As For Me
and My House*. Ross tells us that *Whir of Gold* began as a short
story which he revised and extended. Originally it was the story of
Mad. When, in the course of revision he made Sonny the narrator,
Sonny developed into the central character.[1] The genesis of the
work recalls the process by which *As For Me and My House*,
originally planned with Philip Bentley as protagonist, became
centered upon Mrs. Bentley.

Sonny McAlpine is the prairie farm boy of Ross's story "The
Outlaw." Sonny, a clarinetist who has moved to Montreal to further
his career, is disappointed at his lack of success in the city.
Discouraged, homesick, and almost penniless, he is on the verge of
giving up and returning West, to his limited success as a small-town
band-leader. Trying to stave off loneliness on a Saturday night he
wanders into a nightclub to listen to the band. Here he meets Mad,
a Nova Scotian as lonely as Sonny. Mad is immediately attracted to
Sonny and, after spending the night with him, moves into his sleazy
room to look after him. Sonny's only other acquaintance is a small-
time crook named Charlie who lives across the hall. Sonny's affair
with Mad, the struggle between Mad and Charlie for Sonny, and
Sonny's internal conflict concerning a proposed robbery provide the
central issues of the novel.

Structurally, *Whir of Gold* reverses the situation in *The Well*. In
the earlier novel the young urban criminal is redeemed by nature;
here the young prairie boy is corrupted by the city. In *The Well*
Larson and Sylvia struggle for Chris. In *Whir of Gold* Mad and
Charlie struggle for Sonny, but this time the woman is on the side
of generosity and kindness, the man the representative of evil.

Charlie wins, temporarily, when he persuades Sonny to join him in a holdup. However, Sonny is injured in the course of the robbery and Charlie then vindicates Mad's opinion of him by deserting with the loot. When Sonny's gunshot wound becomes infected Mad locates a doctor who not only treats the wound but provides a contact for a job in a band. Mad nurses Sonny back to health, then, sensing his rejection, leaves.

I   *The Saskatchewan Past*

The action takes place in Montreal in midwinter within a period of three to four weeks. The novel is told retrospectively as Sonny, in an attempt to understand events and his own role in them, relives these weeks in his own mind. It is shot through with scenes from Sonny's prairie childhood: his musical hopes, his first sexual experience, and his adventure with the horse, Isabel. Music and the spirited horse provide stimuli to the boy's imaginative life in an otherwise bleak environment. Sonny's reminiscences most often take him back to Isabel:

> One horse and all horses—somehow representative. Chargers, mustangs, Arabians, standing beside her in the stall, I knew and rode them all. In the neigh and eyes and forelock there was history. Battle and carnage, trumpets and glory—she understood and carried me triumphantly.
> She was coal-black, gleaming, queenly. Her mane had a ripple and her neck an arch. And somehow, softly and mysteriously, she was always burning. The reflection on her glossy hide, sun or lantern, seemed the glow of some secret passion. There were moments when you felt the whole stable charged with her, as if she were the priestess of her kind, in communion with her deity.[2]

To readers of "The Outlaw" these words will sound familiar. The description of Isabel is given here in almost the same words as in that story.[3] Isabel represents the more exciting aspect of Sonny's personality—that which makes him feel he is different, superior, destined for success. Something of the arrogance and pride he sees in Isabel's temperament is in fact a projection of his own arrogance and pride.

Significantly, Isabel and music, the two loves of Sonny's childhood, coalesce in the single most striking incident of the novel, the horse race, which Ross situates exactly in the middle of the novel. Young Sonny defies his parents' prohibition and enters Isabel

in a race at the town fair, certain that she will win. She does win and
the prize provides the needed money for Sonny's music lessons. The
incident also earns Sonny the friendship and support of the local
band-leader, Larry Turnbull, who observes the race.

This self-contained incident possesses the characteristics we are
accustomed to finding in Ross's short stories: humor, economy,
skillful combination of dialogue with retrospective narration, and an
introductory conversation which leads directly into the action. In
this instance, the initial conversation is an argument between
thirteen-year-old Sonny and his mother: "I say so and your father
says so—*that's* who says so. For the last time, you're not riding her
in any race. Not if there was a chance of winning a *thousand*
dollars" (96). The action, compressed into six pages, encompasses
the boy's debate with his mother, his lighthearted ride into town on
Isabel, complications involving his entry into the race, and the race
with its results. Throughout this adventure Isabel remains her
cocky, assured self, a fitting ally for her confident young rider.

The boy's disobedience of his parents' injunction and his
lies—about Isabel's previous racing experience and his parents' permission to race—indicate the strength of his determination to have
a musical career, and foreshadow his adult rejection of moral values
in the name of the same ambition.

Isabel remains a source of inspiration to the adult Sonny. Struggling home alone and wounded from the holdup, floundering and
falling in the snow, Sonny relives another childhood incident in
which Isabel had tossed him into a snowbank.[4] In his confused state
of mind he merges present and past, and as he forces himself to
struggle on he hears Isabel urging him: "And Isabel too joined in.
'That's right, before you freeze to death . . . stand up and walk,
stand up and walk—' " (148).

While Isabel is a stimulus to his imaginative life, Dorothy Whittle, the small-town music teacher, provides a more prosaic example
of a positive influence from Sonny's childhood. The portrayal of
Dorothy is both amusing and compassionate. Her eccentric
behavior and oddities of dress are revealed in a few brief descriptive
passages; for example, Dorothy's "grey tweed coat with a bit of rab-
bity fur around the collar and a hat ablaze with yellow daisies" (73)
suggests the two sides of her personality: the "grey tweed coat", an
indication of her mundane, practical nature, and the hat "ablaze
with yellow daisies" of that vitality which Sonny describes as "a
spark, an urgency, an area of rapture" (73).

The account of Sonny's music lessons provides an amusing demonstration of small-town bickering:

> Lessons were in the dining room of the Metropolitan Hotel. At one time Mrs. Riley, the veterinary's wife, had placed her living room at Dorothy's disposal—her contribution to the town's cultural flowering: and in return (lunch and dinner were also included) Dorothy had paid Mrs. Riley five dollars in cash and given free lessons to her two daughters. But with small-town inevitability, word got back to Dorothy that Mrs. Riley had remarked at choir practice it was little wonder Dorothy's husband had disappeared with another woman; the mystery was how any man with that much enterprise and gumption had taken up with such a dreary piece of teeth and leather in the first place. In response to which Dorothy, while informing parents and pupils that lessons would henceforth be given in the Metropolitan, let it be known that the Riley girls had repeatedly taken peppermints and silver from her purse, and hinted that only the bits and pieces collected by a veterinary in the course of his professional duties could account for the frequency and flavour of Mrs. Riley's stews.
>
> And yet there was a spark, an urgency, an area of rapture. She couldn't play Beethoven but she knew how he should be played. And somehow, entreaty, temper, tears—plus hours, I would swear to it, on her knees—she somehow whipped me into shape to enter the provincial festival with one of the early sonatas and carry it off with a resounding ninety-nine. (73)

Sonny's mother, now dead, remains a major force in his life. When Sonny says, on the first page of the novel, "There were even times when I wished my mother out of the way. Lie down and turn over, I'd say. Stop showing your hands," he is underlining a whole area of his past which continues to influence his present. He adds, "She had been a help at first, an ally, the hands pointing the way I knew I ought to go. 'Make something of yourself, Sonny. Don't go soft—don't come down to their level. All these years it's what I've lived and worked for.'" Sonny will continue throughout the novel to recall his mother and her pervasive and continuing influence for, as he says himself, "She was there. Like a fly in the ear, too deep for match or pin. As if, instead of putting her into her coffin, they had buried her inside me" (3). His mother's influence is ambivalent: in his mind he hears her urging him to success and then, when he desperately concludes that any way to achieve it, even Charlie's way, is justified, she reminds him of his staunchly moral upbringing. Sonny claims, for example, that "It was because of her, in fact, that I met Mad. Objecting to Charlie—Charlie and his offer of a dirty job—that was what finally drove me out" (3). Sonny, then, links his dreams of a musical career with three female figures from his past: his mother, his eccentric small-town music teacher, and an unpredictable, insolent thoroughbred mare. With so many references to Saskatchewan, flashbacks to incidents there, and use of prairie imagery, Saskatchewan is as integral to the novel as Montreal. Transitions from Montreal to Sonny's prairie childhood provide a change of tempo and in most instances a lightening of mood; and the contrast with his present dreary life in a bleak Montreal rooming house helps to explain his homesickness and disappointment. Sonny seems to come alive in these reminiscences, and as a result Saskatchewan is more vividly portrayed than Montreal.

In a number of Montreal experiences Sonny's behavior parallels that in his boyhood, indicating that "The child is father of the man."[5] His unthinking cruelty in trapping the flicker parallels the unthinking cruelty of his actions to Mad. His sexual initiation with Millie, whom he exploits, is similar to his interlude with Mad: in neither relationship is there any indication of genuine affection on his part. His rejection of Mad's warnings about Charlie recalls his disobedience of his parents' instructions about the race. Ironically, in both instances an unexpected benefit is a meeting with someone connected with a band.

II *The Artist*

The first serious assessment of Sonny's musical ability was given by the music festival adjudicator who recognized the inadequacy of Sonny's training and warned the boy that, although he had won the competition, he was late in developing his talents. Sonny said, "I think what you really mean, I'm running too late," (76) and not long after that, he accepted the fact thathis family would never be able to provide the training essential to become a concert pianist. He set his sights lower—to Larry Turnbull's band—and the clarinet. For Sonny this compromise is more acceptable because he has chosen an elite instrument, one which presents more of a challenge than other band instruments.

Sonny, like Philip Bentley, represents the struggling artist. Like Philip he is a lonely figure lacking the stimulus or the opportunity for development of his talent. Like Philip he must struggle against the poverty and isolation of his prairie environment. Like young Tom Dickson in "Cornet at Night," Sonny had his mother's support, although she lacked understanding of the true nature of his ambition: "Had she known that lessons were going to lead to fugues and sonatas instead of 'Trees' and 'Danny Boy' she might not have made such a fierce stand in the first place against my father's disapproval" (73). Despite Dorothy Whittle's efforts, his own hard work, and Isabel's winnings, Sonny did start too late, and he lacked the funds for advanced study. Thus he provides another example of the Canadian artist without the necessary milieu and support for development of his talent. Nevertheless music remains Sonny's world. After his initial success with the Saskatchewan band he had expected that in the Eastern urban centers he would find, "A clean, brave, honest world, where men and clarinets alike received their due" (10). But now he realizes that life is not that simple and bitterly recalls his decision to play the clarinet, to salvage what he could of his dream of a musical career:

What a laugh for Dorothy if she knew? It had been such a solemn decision to make the compromise, step down from the heights to play the clarinet—to play it in a dance band. Bestowal, consent—like a plain, good girl resolving in great moral torment not to hoard her treasure, and then discovering that nobody wants it, not even offered free.

A double compromise: one foot in and the other out again. It was the practical streak that had finally got the better of Dorothy and her exhortations to do as the upwards-striving fish had done; but it was a furtive loyalty to the old belief—a relapse—that had nosed me towards the clarinet. Quality: from the very first I knew. There was Larry, of course, to teach and persuade me, to say why not? what have you got to lose? But any other instrument and I would probably have tired of it within a week. For the clarinet meant salvage: bits and pieces from the ruins big enough to glue. The negative of the dream: scratched and smudged a bit, but go ahead anyway. Develop it and see what's there. Popular and blues—Mozart and Brahms—there were roads in all directions.

Isabel, though, not Dorothy, was to blame for the condescension with which I yielded, for the upstart insolence. Dorothy was a fool—big enough for even me to see. Isabel, in contrast, was wily, hard—the disdain and intolerance of a thoroughbred. "Larry Turnbull Number Two? It's entirely up to you. But if you have other plans, get on with them. The bigger the better—nothing half way. The sooner the better, too, or you'll be runniing late again." (81 - 82)

III   *The Robbery*

Several events come together to bring forth Sonny's capitulation to Charlie. He has just been rejected by a sleazy East-end club for which the clarinet is too refined; and his old arrogance reasserts itself as he rages at the further step "down from the heights" which he must now take to play the saxophone, a lesser instrument. Also, Charlie has succeeded in revealing Mad to him at her most vulgar and most possessive; his sense of shame at accepting Mad's support leads him in two directions—to a determination to get money somehow to repay her, and to a hopeless sense that he has sunk so low that "it was clear now—what I was, what I had become. Therefore nothing mattered. Therefore I was justified" (103).

Yet, Sonny can never clearly account for taking this step into crime, and he attempts to explain it in metaphoric terms:

> There must have been a moment when the key clicked and turned—a moment of decision, involving *me*—but when I go back I find only the door, first closed, then open, never the act of opening it.
> There must have been a path or trail of some sort, firm beneath me all the way; but trying to retrace my steps, to part the bushes and jump the rocks, is like trailing an unknown quarry whose tracks suddenly disappear and then, away on, resume; as if it had wings or were capable of enormous leaps—some kind of monster kangaroo.
> Less leap, though, than suspension. Common sense, ambition, the way I had been brought up—everything said *no:* I knew better. I had a clarinet and a future—a stake in going straight. But there was a break, a blackout, a dead path—almost as if I had been slipped a drug.
> A temporary derangement, then, brought on by worry and depression. Paralysis and flap. Things were too much for me. I cracked and jammed. (114)

The repetition of "There must have been. . . ," "There must have been," and the incantatory rhythm as in "to retrace my steps, to part the bushes, and jump the rocks," echo Sonny's own fruitless searching over and over within himself for an explanation. The staccato sentences of the last two paragraphs reflect his disconnected thought processes as he stumbles from one possible explanation to another, and also his heightened emotional state.

In retrospect Sonny is unable to explain what it was like in that alien world in which he found himself, on the other side of the law: "What was it like out there? And still again, why?

But I, who have made the trip and crossed the border, come back with blank pages" (121).

To Sonny it seems that in committing this crime he has stumbled into a totally different world, "a looking glass world" (128). That his own criminal action seems unreal to him is confirmed by his later

words equating the holdup with a drama, in which he felt like a last
minute substitute playing a part which is not right for him:

> It went like the performance of a well-rehearsed play in which I was a
> last-minute substitute. I had been told the action, given my lines, and now
> I walked on blindly, dazed, to find every movement expected and respond-
> ed to. It wasn't quite real; I didn't quite believe it. Therefore I felt no par-
> ticular concern about the outcome. It was only a role; therefore there was
> no danger. The trouble was the role itself; it wasn't right for me, and I was
> certain to handle it badly. Something like wearing clothes that   don't
> belong to you, don't fit. I was more embarrassed than afraid. (138)

Yet Sonny ultimately refuses to accept his own excuses for his
part in the holdup—and although he is never able to explain
satisfactorily to himself why he made the leap from ordinary, law-
abiding citizen to criminal, he admits responsibility for it: "Circles.
I don't know. Perhaps in every lapse there is a step, blind and unwilling, that springs the trap. Perhaps no man, the tangle of his
fears and hungers bared, is guilty. But the old Presbyterian streak
survives, and I don't get away with that one either. Nonresponsibili-
ty stands up to it like a cotton shirt to a prairie blizzard. Morally, I
take my medicine" (114).

When he decided to join Charlie, Sonny rationalized his involvement in the robbery as an act of daring of which Isabel would approve, and went so far as to tell himself that once he had succeeded
his parents, too, would approve—as once they had approved his
riding Isabel against their commands. As he tries to keep up his
courage prior to the robbery he repeatedly refers to his own sure-
footedness in following the path he has chosen:

> You did what you could, put your feet where there was firm footing. The
> ground varied, smooth and rocky, bog and sand. The feet were always
> yours.
>   And I had good feet. On the way up you couldn't afford to be finicky
> about where you put them. Good feet and a fair share of guts.
> Tonight—with Charlie—that was going to take guts, wasn't it? (127).

Such meanderings confirm the confusion in his mind, for up to this
point in the narrative Sonny has spoken not of his good feet but of
the clumsiness of his "big prairie feet," which militates against
creating a favorable impression in job interviews. It is appropriate
that when his venture into crime ends disastrously, the bullet strikes
his foot; and as he come floundering and stumbling home to Mad,

he finds that he has neither the good feet nor the firm footing he had tried to persuade himself were his.

IV   *The Whir of Gold*

Sonny's musical ambition is symbolized by a childhood experience with a flicker. He recalls catching glimpses of the bird "flashing like a whir of gold, a gust of feathered light." Entranced by its beauty he unthinkingly set a trap for it, hoping "to run the miracle to earth, lay hands on it, for all time make it mine" (162):

> A kind of make-believe—perhaps that would explain it. The trap was all I had, all I could think of. I no more expected to catch the flicker than a dog, bursting from a farmyard in furious pursuit, expects to catch the passing car.
>
> But half an hour later there it was. Head down, suspended by the chain, its leg mangled, its wings flapping feebly, ruffled and bruised. And the eye, just about level with mine, an unsparing, snake-hard little drill of hate. (163)

This incident with the flicker is central to the novel. Sonny's behavior in this episode is analogous to his present behavior with Mad and his participation in the robbery, which he attempts to rationalize as assertions of his freedom, attempts to shake off restraints and express himself. But living on the money of a goodhearted prostitute who loves him, and participating in the holdup of an old man, are less attractive occupations than he has been prepared to admit. He has done these things because of his eagerness to possess and delight in the beauty of music.

By situating this experience from Sonny's boyhood as a dream occurring shortly after the robbery, Ross makes the connection between the two events quite obvious. In a semidelirium caused by his infected wound, Sonny dreams of the bird, of his attempt to capture the "whir of gold." Wakening from his dream he hears again his brother's words of disgust at his action mingling with Mad's words about Charlie, "dirty and cheap. And that'll be you, too, dirty and cheap, just as long as you keep knowing him" (160). At this moment, as he links the two deeds in his mind, he awakens psychologically to the reality of what he has done:

> "Dirty and cheap—dirty and cheap—there'll be no more roses for you."
> Awake and not quite awake: the eye kept shining through the darkness and at the same time burning hot within me like a coal. "Catch and

kill—cheap cheap cheap. Big-time Sonny and his name in lights—no more roses, no more gold—" (163).

The words with which Sonny recalls his own action in trapping the flicker, "A kind of make-believe—perhaps that would explain it," remind the reader of his earlier attempt to explain his role in the robbery, "It wasn't real, I didn't quite believe it." Just as he was unable to realize the implication of his deed until after he had trapped the flicker, so it is only after the robbery and its consequences that he comes to grips with his own culpability. This ability to dissociate himself from his own actions carries over to his behavior with Mad, whom he looks upon as a real person only when she is leaving him.

V *Sonny and Mad*

Mad, a big, generous hearted, irrepressible woman, is not a complex character. Like Sonny she is the product of a simple, rural environment. Sonny noted that "On the farm you count. There are so few of you—you feel known and watched. Afterwards you never quite come to terms with crowds and anonymity" (11); at their first meeting Mad reflects a similar reaction to the city, "You don't know yet how much nobody cares" (17).

Since her first romance at sixteen Mad continues to search for another "right one," someone who will bring back a little of that same feeling she had with her first love, Bill, whom she has idealized in her memories: "I used to meet him up the shore a piece—rocks and an old boat and a nice little place in the sand—and I'd be there first and watch him coming, straight out of the sun when it was starting to set and all the light on him. I don't know how to tell it—sort of like a dream coming true. Crazy as crazy, but coming true" (25). Theirs was a shortlived affair, and since then even a fleeting affair with a "right one" seems worthwhile, a way of making the dream come true again, at least for the moment. There has been a parade of "right ones" since Bill.

There are a number of parallels between the situations of Sonny and Mad. For both of them, their affair provides a temporary bulwark against the future. Ross indicates the similarity of their dilemmas by using the same images—of the curtain and the dirty windowpane—to convey the feelings of both. Sonny says:

I wanted it to last, to stretch pleasure like a curtain and shut out the day and week ahead; but making it last is for the ageing and the jaded, for mortals, and I gave myself without restraint or calculation. Largess befitting the rank to which she had raised me, a reckless fling as if I were born to it and need never stint myself or think about tomorrow: then lying back exhausted with an empty purse. The curtain fell. The glass behind it was as cracked and dirty as I feared. (31)

Mad, too, as she thinks of the future "looked bleak a moment—a cold, early-morning look through a dirty windowpane" (18). She, too, is seen as "taut, guarded, as if she too were holding up a curtain" (33).

The image of the fish provides another link between them. Dorothy Whittle compared young Sonny with his talent to "an insane fish—. . . . One that wouldn't stay in the sea where it belonged and insisted on climbing up the rocks and onto the shore. . . . Just remember that you, too, can do the impossible" (72). When he says to Mad "You're not just a fish, Mad—you're an *insane* fish," he adds, remembering Dorothy's words and his own experience, "Fins won't do—you've got to have legs. Me, too—a long time ago—only I was smarter. Didn't take so long to learn it's rough going for a fish on shore. . . ." (71). But Mad's reply, "Sure I'm a fish—Mad the Tuna—sure I'm crazy—but I'm getting something I'd never have got if I always watched and played it careful" (77), suggests her difference from Sonny who, having given up his impossible dream, admits "It was the practical streak that had finally got the better of Dorothy and her exhortations to do as the upwards-striving fish had done" (81).

Mad's love for Sonny is a combination of motherly devotion and sexual need. Her generosity makes him feel guilty, her cooking and mothering lead him to feel trapped, and her joy in his sexual performance confirms his view of himself as a gigolo. His frequent reminders of the impermanence of their relationship cannot deter Mad from speaking hopefully of a future together operating a little restaurant in Nova Scotia. Sonny, himself, sees that "her chances with me were like mine with Beethoven and a career" (123). But Mad, he insists, must make a compromise with her dream as he has done:

And hadn't I been fair? Right from the start hadn't I told her what she could expect? If she picked the wrong "right one" and suffered for it was it anybody's fault but her own? After all, you've got to take your own measure, come to terms with what you are. It's easy to want, to dream; the pinch is adjusting to what you have a right to. Jazz and the blues in exchange for the other—what I really wanted—that hadn't been easy either. Hadn't been—*wasn't*. For you don't get away with a couple of bad days, a single wrench of renunciation. The ghost of a might-have-been goes with you all the way, clinging to your back like an Old Man of the Sea, sneering at the deal you made. Even though it was the only possible deal this side of lunacy—still there's the whisper, "What was the hurry? How could you have been so sure? Supposing you had given yourself another ten years—supposing you'd been right all along—" (123 - 24).

Sonny's sensitivity and Presbyterian background combine to torture him with a sense of guilt about his treatment of Mad who is, after all, in love with him: ". . . it was as if I too were something coming true, coming towards her, incredible and unknown, with a swing of light around my shoulders. A swan, a bull, a shower of gold" (31). The words "shower of gold" link Sonny with the flicker. He is Mad's "whir of gold," the transitory beauty, the dream that can never come true. At the same time this description of Mad's initial reaction to Sonny links him with Bill, her first love, whom she recalled earlier, "coming, straight out of the sun . . . and all the light on him. I don't know how to tell it—sort of like a dream coming true" (25). For Sonny, Mad has been a temporary refuge, their relationship an attempt to stave off loneliness for the moment, "to shut out the day and week ahead." His final act of cruelty to her is an effort to make their break easier for her. As such, it differs from his treatment of the flicker which he lacked the courage to destroy after disabling, and thus may indicate some movement on his part toward maturity and responsibility.

Ironically, at this last moment Sonny sees Mad in a different light. She steps out of the stereotyped role in which he has always viewed her and becomes an individual to him through the simple expedient of changing her fussy dress for a simpler one. Her role changes with this change of clothing: ". . . it made her intact, gave her identity. Until now she had been just a sprawl of a woman—wanton, overwhelming, all impulse and devotion; but now, encased not so much in the dress as in its simplicity, she seemed suddenly to have gathered herself together, to have withdrawn, taken shape. Different—something that hadn't been there before, a new dimension. Just when she was walking out on me" (191).

At the end of the novel Mad leaves with her dream still intact. No doubt she will go on looking for another "right one." Sonny's dreams, in contrast, have all turned to nightmares. His dream of capturing the whir of gold became the nightmare of the mangled bird; his dream of a musical career has brought him to the reality of a cheap Montreal boardinghouse and a chance at playing saxophone; and his dream of a temporary respite with Mad has ended with an awareness of what he may have missed: "—but for a long time, streets and days, I heard the footsteps. 'Sonny and Mad—they got a nice swing. Listen now—sort of go together. Sonny and Mad—Sonny and Mad—just like it was intended' " (195).

VI Style and Narrative Technique

The first person narrative gives the reader the restricted viewpoint of Sonny McAlpine. Sonny, aware in himself of the pressure of his past on his present, of the clash of Mad's, Charlie's, his mother's, his teacher's, Isabel's influences on his behavior, can only guess at the motives of the other characters. Because of this limited point of view, Mad and Charlie must share past experiences with Sonny so that the reader, as well as Sonny, can have some insight into their nature.

Although the narration is retrospective, the reader is given the illusion of immediacy, of being himself present in the scene of the remembered action. Dialogue, used extensively, adds to the immediacy. The illusion of reality is heightened by Ross's dramatic method whereby he presents brief scenes designed to intensify mood and reveal character rather than merely further the action. Exposition and description, filtered through Sonny's mind, unfold unobtrusively. His description of his room, of the basement hall where he applies for a job, of other characters, is presented in conjunction with his reactions to them and provides a sense of the dramatic present. Each character speaks in a distinctive way. Mad's simplified diction and grammatical errors add to her portrait as exuberant and well-meaning but not particularly bright. Her loquaciousness is made evident by the dreary repetitiousness of her remarks.

One problem in the novel, apart from the occasional overelaborate metaphor, lies in a structural imbalance. For although the story, ostensibly that of Sonny and Mad, does begin with their meeting and end with their parting, the central tension is more directly concerned with the holdup—the concatenation of events leading to Sonny's capitulation to Charlie, his rationalizations, then his desperate flight and the dilemma posed by his injury—rather than his relationship with Mad.

The tempo of the novel varies. As with *The Well* Ross selects specific incidents within the timespan of a few weeks to recount in detail. For example when time is slowed for the robbery the vivid detailing of the final preparations and of Sonny's emotional reactions heightens the suspense. It is also "slowed" for Sonny's long drawn out flight, and for the final quarrel between Sonny and Mad. Much like Dostoevski, Ross presents at a slow pace and in detail the conflicting emotions, the rationalizations, and the disordered thoughts that lead to Sonny's ultimate decision to participate in the holdup.

The novel, which begins in a reminiscent mood, gradually draws the reader into the narrative and into the chronological presentation of events which begins in the second chapter. The final lines of the novel, as Mad's footsteps echo down the stairway for the last time, take the reader back to the beginning by repeating virtually the same words with which the novel began: "Sonny and Mad—they got a nice swing. Listen now—sort of go together. Sonny and Mad—Sonny and Mad—just like it was intended" (195). The reader finds himself drawn back from the present into the past, recalling the experiences and emotions just relived with Sonny, and the hauntingly reminiscent mood with which the novel began.

Throughout *Whir of Gold* the central tension within Sonny is that evoked by opposing aspects of his past: his Presbyterian upbringing and practical farmer's background in conflict with the imagination and daring represented by Isabel. Thus he is continually torn between discipline and release, practicality and imagination, caution and daring. Boyhood experiences on the prairies developing these tensions are called back into his mind during these few weeks in a rundown Montreal rooming house. He views his decision about his musical career as a compromise between the two ever present polarities in his life: Dorothy and Isabel urging him on and his practical Saskatchewan upbringing requiring him to face reality: "And there was a shrewd practical streak. Sacrifices were fine, so long as they led somewhere. Like a good farmer, I had an eye for yield" (76). Despite the Montreal setting Sonny remains psychologically in Saskatchewan. His judgments continue to be influenced by Isabel or Dorothy or his mother. Sonny is judged by the reader not solely by virtue of the few incidents occurring within these few weeks. His

life, and even Charlie's and Mad's lives, are viewed in the light of
their past which has largely determined their outlook and personality.

The two levels of time are equally present in Sonny's mind, his
formative childhood years and the present moment. At one point, in
fact, three levels of time come together—remote past, immediate
past, and present—all in retrospect—which makes actually a fourth
time level, the present moment. This coming together of four levels
of time occurs in the central incident in which, a couple of days
after the robbery, as Sonny dreams of the flicker of his childhood,
he thinks at the same time of Mad's warning about Charlie a week
or so earlier, linking the two examples of his own meanness; these
recollections occur at a particular moment after the holdup which
he is now recalling. This multilevel use of time is important to
demonstrate that Sonny is a product of his past, and to show him
reaching some degree of self-understanding by relating the two
events in his mind.

Prairie imagery permeates the novel, and its use in the Montreal
setting is another device linking Montreal and Saskatchewan. For
example, the planned holdup: "like a barn in a blizzard, was just
there, just a blur, just visible" (125); and Sonny's denial of responsibility stands up against his Presbyterian conscience "like a cotton
shirt to a prairie blizzard" (114). Occasionally the imagery seems
overly elaborate and contrived, as in this reflection: "If you could
only know: see a here-and-now for what it was, how it fitted in, its
place in the terrain of your existence: a sloughbottom on the
prairie—as little as that—or a dip to a lost valley, descent of no
return" (26).

Sonny most frequently sees Mad in terms of hunting, in an image
effectively combining his sense of her helplessness and his own
guilt: "For someone like me she was a gift—a hen for a coyote. Silly
hens that went wandering—wasn't that how coyotes lived?" (57)
He returns in thought to the same image on their last day together:

One of the best—big-hearted, warm. Even tactful, careful never to remind me she went out to work and buy the steaks while I slept late and
played the clarinet; everything on the credit side but her headful of damfool ideas about a right one some day who would last. And at that, not able
to tell the difference: a real right one or a real rat. Not able to understand
that for someone like her there are only rats, just as for a hen that goes
walking across the prairie, there are only hawks and coyotes. (183)

In relation to Mad, Sonny sees himself as the hunter, "I leaned a little on the last words and then watched to see if they had got
through, the same as I would watch sometimes, the rifle still at my
shoulders, to see if I had got my rabbit" (70). Yet at the same time
he fears the reverse, the possibility of being trapped into a commitment to her: "But the dollar she had left—and my hand so ready,
unconcerned. A flash of panic as I caught myself, a sudden lost feeling, as if a lever had been pulled, a trap sprung. . . . (53). Similarly
although he uses the image of the hunter in referring to the planned
holdup, "like trailing an unknown quarry" (114), afterwards, alone,
ill, and terrified, the situation is reversed and he sees himself no
longer the hunter but the hunted:

A cornered rabbit, no place to run. . . .
    And like a rabbit I could only run. Nothing to fight with; no defences.
Cornered. Nothing but to wait till they closed in for the kill. . . .
    And the pain now, purring like a motor, driving me. Nowhere to run, and
driving me. Pacing—the pain squelching up every time I brought my foot
down as if I had stepped into a puddle of it, and yet pacing. Foot and
teeth—a grinding itch in the teeth to bite it out, like a weasel in a trap trying to gnaw off its leg— (167).

The short, sharp phrases, the repetition, the images of entrapment
and desperation and pain combine to intensify the sense of terror
and heighten the impression of mounting hysteria. There are
numerous instances throughout the novel of such correlation of
rhythm with the emotional impact which the words themselves seek
to convey. In the following sentence, for example, the incantatory
rhythm combines with repetition of the word "grubby" to underline the dreary inevitability of Mad's future: "The years ahead,
the grubby rooms and the grubby friends and the grubby bars,
clothes starting to scuff, face starting to sag—from the brave, silly
babble you could chart her course as easily as an expert in such
things could chart the trajectory of a missile" (156). The parallel of
the "trajectory of a missile" with Mad's future underlines the inevitability of her fate, and also suggests that someone is responsible
for setting her course, just as someone charts the course of a missile.
The evasive "an expert in such things" avoids consideration of Sonny's responsibility in charting her course. In itself, the missile image
is yet another indication that Sonny is viewing Mad as less than a
human being. Only when she is leaving does he see her step out of
her stereotyped role as "a sprawl of a woman."

VII   *Conclusion*

Whir of Gold is a mood story.   The questioning, the introspection,
the richly metaphorical language, and the haunting sense of guilt
and regret are conveyed in a tightly knit narrative of three alienated
people.
The whir of gold symbolizes a fleeting, elusive beauty, a dream.
To attempt to capture and make it permanent is to destroy it as the
flicker's beauty was destroyed in the trap.   For Sonny, the elusive
beauty is music and his musical career; the means he uses to try to
capture it are as thoughtless and cruel as his gopher trap and
ironically cause his own entrapment.   Mad's dream is the romantic
one of a permanent "right one"; her attempts to achieve this
dream, as represented by Sonny, end in disappointment.   Charlie's
dream of achieving self-importance as a successful criminal has kept
him on the run for twenty years, his only satisfaction now found in
reducing others to his own level.   Ross seems to be saying that the
attempt "to run the miracle to earth, lay hands on it, for all time
make it mine" brings only disillusion, pain, despair.   To catch a
glimpse from time to time of this "whir of gold" is all one can expect in this world.   To possess it forever is beyond man's reach.   To
attempt to trap it is to be entrapped oneself.   Ross was right to
change the title from the originally conceived *Sonny and Mad*[6] to
Whir of Gold, which better conveys the central focus, while at the
same time including the Mad-Sonny relationship.   *Whir of Gold* is a
haunting, memorable, finely crafted novel, reminiscent in subtlety
and economy of language of *As For Me and My House*.   Particularly
in its manipulation of time it is a major step forward for Ross.

CHAPTER 6

Sawbones Memorial

IN *Sawbones Memorial* Sinclair Ross returns to the prairie
setting of his earlier stories and novels to take the reader once
more through the pioneer days, the depression, and the drought.

On April 20, 1948, "Sawbones" Hunter is retiring after forty-five
years in Upward, Saskatchewan. Townspeople who have gathered
to honor him mingle and recall the past. Although the action of the
novel takes place within a few hours, Ross, through the thoughts
and memories of those present, skillfully manipulates time to reveal
four generations. For the most part, setting is limited to the lounge
of the new Hunter Memorial Hospital where the festivities are being held. The only piece of furniture of significance in this innocuous setting is the piano which had belonged to Doc's wife and
which, like the old songs played on it, provides one of the leitmotifs
of the novel and one of the links with past and future. Since the
evening is to include the official opening of the hospital named in
Doc's honor, as well as bidding farewell to Doc, the scene is well
designed for reminiscence and, at the same time, as talk turns in-
evitably to the new building and even more to the new doctor—for
considering the future as well. Time stands still as past and future
come together in the present moment.

Composed solely of dialogue and monologue, this is Ross's most
innovative novel. Ross's techniques and principles of organization
derive from cinema and music. Each of the many voices in the
novel is an instrument through which he orchestrates his various
themes; verbal refrain, leitmotifs, and recurrent imagery contribute
to the creation of a novel which resembles a musical score. Techniques of modern cinema such as flashback, closeup, cutting, and
fadeout also contribute to Ross's expression.

I   *Structure*

The novel is composed of forty individual episodes which vary in length from a few lines to twelve pages, including six interior monologues, two speeches, one dramatic monologue, snatches of conversation, and more extended conversations between two or more individuals. Although there is no psychological progression in the characters there is a gradual revelation of the different personalities. The novel is carefully patterned so that our understanding of each individual grows gradually as his name is mentioned from time to time in conversation or thought until in many cases we meet him in one of the conversational groups.

The internal structure of the novel is cyclic. The time is spring, the date April 20—the date Doc began his practice at Upward and now the date of his leaving it. As Doc retires, young Dr. Miller is beginning, and he is returning to the town of his birth which he had left years earlier. The celebration itself, a farewell to Doc and official opening of Hunter Memorial Hospital, is an event which both looks back on Doc's forty-five years here, and looks forward to the modern hospital and Nick Miller ushering in a new era. As Doc says in the concluding section of the novel, "It's all over and it's all beginning, there's nothing more required of you. April and the smell of April, just as it was all beginning that day too. . . ."[1] Ross inextricably unites past and future: Nick is the new doctor; yet, since Nick grew up in Upward, no one can think of him without thinking of the past as well; Hunter Memorial is the name of the new hospital, but its very name calls memory into play, calls up the many years of Doc's practice here. Hunter Memorial is given multiple meanings. Doc jokingly mentions that the cemetery is sometimes called Hunter Memorial. The novel, with its title *Sawbones Memorial*, is itself a memorial to Doc Hunter.

II   *Claude Mauriac and the Nouveau Roman*

Ross has indicated that it was reading Claude Mauriac's *Dîner en ville* (1959)[2] that gave him the idea of writing a novel through the words of a group gathered together for a few hours.[3] Mauriac's *Dîner en ville*, published in English as *Dinner in Town*[4] owes more to the French *nouveau roman* than to the writer's well-known father, novelist François Mauriac. The French New Novelists involved in the evolution of the novel in France since the early 1950's include Alain Robbe-Grillet, Nathalie Sarraute, Michel Butor, and Claude Simon. Vivian Mercier includes Claude Mauriac among the New Novelists[5] although not all critics do. All, however, do agree that he was very much influenced by them. The New Novelists admired and learned from such writers as Kafka, Joyce, Dostoevski, Faulkner, and Proust. Although they differ widely they are united by their rejection of such accepted elements of the novel as plot, setting, conventional narrative method, and character development. They seek to apply methods of poetry, cinema, and music to the novel form.

In Mauriac's *Dîner en ville*, eight individuals are seated around a dining room table in a fashionable Paris apartment overlooking Notre Dame Cathedral. The novel consists entirely of the words and thoughts of the diners. The reader must discover through such clues as characteristic words and phrases, and with the help of a seating plan provided, who is speaking or whose thoughts are being revealed. There is no introduction of characters, no direct description, no narrative intervention. There is little overt action; the novel begins as the guests enter the dining room and ends as dinner is concluded. Through the words and thoughts of these eight people their hopes, ambitions, fears, intrigues, and interrelationships are revealed. One of Mauriac's characters says "While dinner lasts we are outside of time." The situation of Ross's characters in *Sawbones Memorial* is similar; they are gathered in a new building, cut off for these few hours from their usual surroundings and activities. They, too, are "outside of time." What Mauriac and Ross have achieved is what Mauriac later calls "the immobilization of time."[6]

In *Dîner en ville* the eight characters are caught in a static situation: throughout the novel they remain seated around the table. *Sawbones Memorial* allows for more fluidity. Ross's characters move about the room, chatting with one person or group and then with another, as conversational groups form, disperse, and reform. Mauriac had been a well-known film critic before becoming a novelist. The influence of film is evident in *Dîner en ville* as he focuses on first one then another individual or duet, and shifts from external dialogue to internal monologue and flashback. Ross's novel allows for an even more flexible cinematic technique, as he cuts back and forth cameralike from group to group and pauses for snatches of conversation, closeups and occasional flashbacks in the form of interior monologues.

Ross recalls that from his first conception of this novel he intended a new building as the setting. Since the Royal Bank in Montreal
where he worked had just completed an impressive new Head Office building he first considered this as a possible locale. Later he
considered a village schoolhouse and then arrived at the idea of the
hospital. Reminiscence is the underlying motive for the use of a new
community building as setting.[7]

III *Characters*

Sawbones Memorial is an expansive novel in which over thirty
characters appear: the old and the young; farmer, teacher,
housewife, and minister; the absent as well as the present; the dead
as well as the living. Ross uses a wide angle lens, crowding his novel
with characters. Beneath the surface he reveals a tumultuous
Dostoevskian activity—including murder, suicide, incest, attempted
rape, abortion, euthanasia—all aspects of the past of this seemingly
ordinary little community disclosed gradually through dialogue and
monologue. So involving is Ross's dialogue that we come to know
those remembered, as well as those present here and now. Thus Ida
Robinson and Edith Hunter and Big Anna, who are dead, and
Maisie Bell and Nick Miller, who are absent, are as integral to the
novel and as real to the reader as Doc Hunter, Harry Hubbs, Duncan and Caroline Gillespie, who are present.

The first lines of the novel initiate the process of movement back
into the past and forward into the future. In a conversation between
Doc and his old friend, Harry Hubbs, we learn that Doc is
celebrating his birthday and his retirement on the same date that he
arrived at Upward. We learn of his genuine concern for his patients
and of his attraction to women. The main characters are mentioned:
Dunc, Caroline, Nick; and Harry and Doc think back to "the old
days," thus setting the reminiscent mood.

Of the characters recalled by the townspeople on this occasion,
the most colorful is Ida Robinson, a determined, domineering
member of the pioneering generation and grandmother of
Upward's leading citizen, Duncan Gillespie. Like Grandmother
MacLeod in Margaret Laurence's *A Bird in the House*, Ida
remembers her superior Ontario upbringing and is not averse to
reminding her family of it: "There had been a seven-roomed house
with a red carpet and white lace curtains in the parlour, beautiful
curtains. . . . There had also been a lawn with lilacs and a pine

tree. . . ." (60). As is true of many of Ross's women, Ida dominates
her weak husband. She finds some consolation and escape from the
rigors of homesteading and a dull husband with young Dr. Hunter,
who also is a newcomer from Ontario. Ida's story is told largely
through her daughter Sarah, town matriarch, now herself a member
of the older generation. Caroline Gillespie, wife of Ida's grandson,
speaks of Ida as one of the mythic characters of the town, a symbol
of Canada's pioneer spirit.

In contrast to Ida, whose hardships and struggles have brought
success to her family and helped to establish this community, old
Harry Hubbs reveals a far different response to the hardships of
homesteading. Harry left his small-town home in Nova Scotia for
the West because of a series of incidents involving horse dealing,
poker, and other men's wives: "I didn't exactly *have* to get out of
town, but I wasn't helping things for my two sisters, both up in
their twenties and starting to worry would anybody want to marry
them. No future for me there anyway, so when the family raked up
a thousand dollars—" (88). As his earlier actions suggest, Harry has
neither the pride nor the stamina to make a homesteader. Although
he arrives in the West with a thousand dollars, a substantial sum of
money in those days, he lacks the will or capacity for hard work.
Ross describes the squalor from which Dr. Hunter rescues this
hapless settler, on the verge of physical and mental collapse. Doc
helps Harry to find a less onerous means of making a livelihood as
watchman at the livery stable. As Harry continues on his irresponsi-
ble way, he expands his activities in the community to include making homebrew, setting up poker games, and pimping for girls he
brings from Regina. "Decadence with one foot in the grave," (80) is
one townsman's description of Harry. Like Doc Hunter, Harry
remains on the periphery of other people's lives.

Most of the interesting characters in this novel are outsiders, and,
from Upward's point of view, anyone who does not adhere to the
town's conventional code is an outsider. Benny Fox, the town musician who grew up with Duncan Gillespie and Nick Miller, is an outsider because of his homosexuality. Benny's mother had been forced
into marriage because of pregnancy and never recovered from the
humiliation. She made life miserable for her quiet, retiring husband
and only son, both of whom she blamed for her predicament. She
dressed Benny in fussy, effeminate clothes—sailor suit, bow tie, and
boater—that made the sensitive child the laughing stock of his
schoolmates. Benny blames his mother, who died of an overdose of

sleeping pills, for his miserable and unbalanced childhood. As a band-leader he is popular and successful. But Doc Hunter warns him now, as he has earlier, to leave Upward and make a new start away from his unhappy memories and from those who remember his family history, to get away before some homosexual incident brings the wrath of the town upon him. Benny is contrasted with Nick Miller, another outsider, but one who did get out of town and make a new life. Nick, too, was derided by his schoolmates because he was different from them, a "hunky" whose mother was a Ukrainian cleaning woman. His reaction was more stoical than Benny's. He left at fifteen, the year his mother died, as soon as he completed high school. Now that Nick is returning as town doctor, it is obvious that Upward still remembers him as "Big Anna's boy," and that a good many of the righteous citizens resent his reappearance in the prestigious role of town doctor. Duncan Gillespie invited Nick to take the position and Doc advised him to accept so that, by returning, he can "lay a few ghosts" (99). "Maybe the best way to get it out of your system is to come back—see it's not worth hating" says Doc, indicating that Nick, like Benny, bears scars from the past.

Caroline Gillespie is the most recent addition to the community. Caroline is an English war bride who married Upward's most eligible young man, Sarah Gillespie's son, Duncan. Stories of early days, especially of Ida Robinson's homesteading experiences and of Doc Hunter's early struggles through blizzards on sick calls, led Caroline to expect a challenging pioneer community: "I wanted so much to be part of it. A big new country, a country of beginnings. I wanted so much to be a pioneer too and do my share" (24). Caroline finds that Upward is not exactly as she had anticipated: "As to the brave new world I was looking for, the country of beginnings, of pioneers—well, last week it was my turn to invite the Ladies' Aid for their weekly meeting, and at four o'clock in the afternoon I served creamed chicken, hot biscuits, ice cream and frozen strawberries—oh yes, and chocolate cake—to about twenty-five women, most of them overweight, all in the name of and to the glory of the Lord" (24 - 25). However, in a different time and different way from Ida, Caroline actually is a pioneer too. She is linked to Ida Robinson by their common struggle to make things grow on the prairie. Coming from Ontario, Ida attempted to grow Manitoba maples and did manage to keep a few scrubby trees alive and to grow a caragana hedge. Coming from a land of ivy and roses, Caroline says:

Yes, the ivy is at least a hundred years old, but there's something to be said too for growing geraniums and begonias in pots. At least for me—you see I used to take the ivy and the roses for granted. Now I have my own ivy, in a pot too, growing like mad. Duncan made me a little trellis, and I'm certainly not taking it for granted. I watch every leaf as if my life depended on it. And my caragana hedge—at least eight inches high. It seems to have stood the winter. (79)

The desire to grow flowers, plants, and hedges and the struggle to keep them alive and flourishing, link both Ida and Caroline with fertility, vitality, and a positive response to life. Caroline will not find her role in Upward easy. She is resented by some of the townspeople for marrying their most prominent citizen and by others for her British origin: "Some of them are starting to say *Her Ladyship*" (76). Yet her status as wife of the community leader requires her to live up to the town's code of behavior.

Maisie Bell is another outsider. Maisie's parlor has been the only hospital Upward has known until today. Yet she is not invited to the official opening of Hunter Memorial. Her kindness to the ill and those in trouble is well known, but suspicion of her immoral behavior with some of Upward's leading citizens puts her beyond the pale. When town journalists Dan and Nellie Frisby decide that Maisie deserves recognition in their paper, Upward meanly objects: "What's so special about keeping clean sheets on four or five beds and emptying a few bed pans?" (105)

Mr. Grimble, the disillusioned Presbyterian minister, calls to mind Philip Bentley of *As For Me and My House*. But now, in 1948, the situation is ironically changed. Where Philip could not accept the religion he himself preached, Mr. Grimble does accept it; but he realizes that now the people themselves, although they maintain the outward forms, no longer believe. Sadly he comments on his own role in Upward: "If I could only believe that despite it all I serve, that some day the seeds will spring and bloom, but I flutter on the margin of their lives, like a leaf that has died and not yet fallen" (73). Grimble's wife is equally discouraged with her role in the community. Her part in this reception indicates her ineffectuality. She has determinedly insisted on a nonalcoholic punch and is unaware that organizers managed to lace the fruit drink with a little rum and gin, although not enough to please those who enjoy alcoholic drinks, including the guest of honor:

Did you try the punch? Just terrible, I know, and such a shame for Doc's party—after all, you're seventy-five only once. Mrs. Grimble, she was the one. You see she's a member of the Auxiliary too and being the preacher's wife sort of gives her some say—nobody feels like talking back. Oh yes, temperance to the eyes. We did slip some gin and rum in, not enough to taste for anybody normal, but she's smacking her lips and saying "Delicious, you see you don't *need* alcohol." (34)

The Grimbles are humorless, deadly serious, and despondent at the failure of their ministry. As comments of the townspeople indicate, they are out of touch with their parishioners, and do indeed, as Grimble says, "flutter on the margin of their lives."

The center of attention on this occasion is Doc Hunter. Because of his profession, he has been involved in most of the crucial events which occurred within the community in the past forty-five years and is aware of most of the skeletons in town closets. Through the variety of viewpoints presented, the reader can make his own assessment of this man who has spent his professional life in Upward. Sarah Gillespie and Harry Hubbs recall Doc's earlier years. Sarah remembers her crush on him when she was a child; Harry recalls Doc's dedicated work during the influenza epidemic and hints at his affairs with lonely wives of tired farmers. "Well, in all modesty," quips Doc, "I think I can say I kept a few out of North Battleford asylum" (9). A somewhat different picture of Doc is given by a woman who bitterly remembers his taking the family calves in payment of overdue bills:

I'll hand it to him the calves and steers were a smart idea. In fact I'd say he missed his calling. Shrewd—what's in it for me? They say he got the land for a song, hilly, not much good for breaking; all he had to do was fence it and put up a windmill. No time at all he had a nice little herd—his 'collections' and the increase. One of the neighbours to keep an eye on things, maybe drop round himself once a month or so. Nothing to do but call in a buyer twice a year and cash his cheques. (75)

The tragedy of Doc's personal life, his unhappy marriage to a frigid wife, is hinted at by a number of townspeople. The loquacious Harry Hubbs reveals that Doc often stayed around the stable playing cards after a sick call rather than returning home to his wife. The town gossips of Doc's attempts to find solace with other women, and especially of his reputed affair with Maisie Bell. Doc helped many with their problems but found no solution for his own. He meditates to himself, "How can you think of someone you marry as a case? You don't hold clinics in the bridal bed" (110). In the first few weeks of his marriage Doc came to realize that his wife's frigidity was more than maidenly modesty: "Night of the moon, the night I saw, and not another word until the day she died, just the weather and the roast, if there are any calls you can tell them I'll be back by three. . . ." (111). Henceforth they lived as strangers in the same house. Doc is a shrewd observer of the human condition. He remains sufficiently removed to recognize the foibles of the town and understand its weaknesses. His tolerance and his sincere attempts to do what is best for individuals regardless of convention contrast with the rigidity and narrowness of the community as a whole.

The townspeople, like a chorus, comment on the action. Many are just as narrow, prejudiced, and hypocritical as Horizon's citizens of the 1930's. Dunc remembers the mean treatment of young Benny Fox and Nick Miller when they were school children. Now many of the same people are behaving in the same way as adults: "This is not a hunky town, Dr. Hunter," says Mrs. Harp, whose husband Ernie had been one of Nick's chief tormentors in childhood, "You don't mind the people you have for friends—you've made that plain over the years—but some of us in Upward are a little more particular. We have a hospital now that's a credit to the town and we want a doctor who's a credit to the hospital. Not Big Anna's boy" (83). This could well be the voice of Horizon's Mrs. Wenderby objecting to Paul Kirby's honesty of expression, notably his use of the word "belly." " 'Cows may have them,' says Mrs. Wenderby, 'and you, Mr. Kirby, but not my daughter Isobel or I' " (70).

As in Horizon, sexual transgression continues to be the most unforgivable sin, especially for a woman. More than twenty years earlier Benny's mother could not live with her sense of shame that the town knew of her misstep. Tonight Maisie Bell is not invited to the hospital opening; for her years of charity to the sick cannot compensate for her reputed affairs with Upward citizens. Benny, popular because of charm and his musical ability, knows that if his homosexuality becomes public the town will turn against him.

Ross develops opposing groups of characters. On the side of life are "Doc" Hunter, Nick Miller, and Maisie Bell who care for the sick and troubled, Ida Robinson and Caroline Gillespie with their enthusiasm for growing things, Benny with his music. In contrast, and often acting in opposition to these, are many of the townspeople: those like Ernie and Mrs. Harp who resent Nick because he is a "hunky," those who will not invite Maisie to the hospital opening, those who criticize Doc for exacting payment from patients, those who resent Caroline because she is a stranger.

IV *Humor*

Sawbones Memorial mingles the tragic with the comic, and reveals man's weaknesses as well as his strengths. It is ultimately more positive than previous Ross works. In keeping with the festivity there is a tendency to interrupt the serious to maintain the relaxed, cheerful atmosphere. The penchant for nostalgic reminiscence is undercut by recollections of amusing incidents. As a result, the element of humor is much more prominent than in earlier works. While Ross's humor is generally ironic, understated, and gentle, in this novel he provides the reader with a broader humor as well.

In one farcical incident proud parents attempt to persuade their five-year-old son to shake hands with the doctor:

"Billy, you hear me! Shake hands! If it wasn't for Dr. Hunter you maybe wouldn't even *be* here."
"Come on, Billy, you want that pony, don't you?"
"Now I'm warning you—for the last time, shake *hands!*"
"That's the way. Wasn't so bad now, was it? And leave your coat alone, we're not going to stay." (29)

In another broadly humorous incident, Benny and an assortment of would-be singers attempt to recall Doc's favorite song, *Redwing*. Each singer responds to the question "Do you know *Redwing?*" with the same words, "Of course I know *Redwing*," but each remembers two different and contradictory lines of the song. They finally resolve the problem by singing the few lines they know and filling in the rest with what they consider to be suitable Indian sounds. During the argument about the words of the song, Nellie Furby makes one of her characteristic quips. In reply to the question "*The sun is shining and Redwing's pining.* Why should she be pining when the sun is shining, what's the connection?" Nellie's response is, "Perhaps it's intended as a comment on the indifference of nature to the human predicament. Very Canadian" (108).

Upward's social pretensions are gently satirized through the dramatic monologue of a Ladies' Auxiliary member, conscious of her position, "Assistant Secretary, I was voted in—" (31), as she shows a young Upward matron around the hospital. The same Ladies' Auxiliary member surfaces again later in a brief dialogue with the hopeful mother of a would-be pianist, to whom she seeks to sell Edith Hunter's piano donated by Doc to the hospital:

"A hundred did you say?"

"*Two* hundred—and a bargain. It hasn't got a scratch."

"If it belonged to his wife it must go back a long way. Two hundred for such an old one seems a lot."

"I've always heard they made them better in the old days. It's a lost art."

"Styles change, though—and it's so big. It seems to me a hundred would be plenty."

"It's a Mason and Risch. That's supposed to be the best."

"My sister has a Heintzman—the one in Medicine Hat."

"Well, your sister's Heintzman in Medicine Hat isn't much help to Joey in Upward, now is it?" (47)

Nellie Furby, the probing newspaperwoman, contributes an astringent wit to her observations of the town. Benny views Upward and his own dilemma with a somewhat more sardonic humor. Doc Hunter's wry comments on the human condition are in keeping with his shrewd but compassionate nature. By juxtaposing humorous with harsher, more serious episodes, and interposing comments by some of the wittier individuals such as Benny, Nellie, and Doc, with more serious conversations and monologues, Ross varies the tone and pace of the novel. For example, a serious dialogue between Doc and Caroline, about the difficulties of earlier years in the community and the disparity between Caroline's expectations and the reality of Upward, is followed by the incident in which embarrassed parents persuade their five-year-old to shake hands with Dr. Hunter.

Doc's own personality and his positive view of reality are the major reasons for the more relaxed tone and therefore the greater element of humor in this novel. Doc faces up to his role as an intelligent being in an unknowable universe and accepts his responsibilities, which he interprets as using his intelligence and skills to serve his community. Doc can ignore the conventions which inhibit Ross's earlier characters and which continue to shackle most of Upward's citizens; therefore he can act decisively, interpreting each situation with love and compassion and acting for the good of the individuals he meets.

V   *Levels of Discourse*

Ross's handling of multiple points of view and different levels of discourse is probably the most outstanding technical accomplishment of this work. The variety of characters provides many opportunities for counterpointing different modes of speech and thought, shifting from the formal to the colloquial, from friendly gossip to bitter accusation, from nostalgic remembrance to guilty regret. Ross also varies the texture of the work by shifting the levels of discourse: from dialogue to interior monologue, from group discussion to dramatic monologue, from formal speech to party chatter. The narrator is a recording consciousness, a camera roving about the surface, exposing this microcosm of the world in an objective, non-judgmental way just as it would appear to the eye and ear of a camera. The reader is allowed to make his own judgments.

Thoughts and emotions are sometimes verbalized as friends and neighbors confess to resentments, jealousies, and affections which the present celebration calls into consciousness. Dialogue emerges like lines spoken in a play, revealing personalities, giving essential information, and contributing to mood. Ross has an excellent ear for speech rhythms and succeeds in giving each character his own distinct and identifiable idiom. The mode of expression varies from the relaxed conversation of friends like Benny, "Boy, was this the life, and was it easy! And Benny Fox from Upward, Saskatchewan, did he know how to handle himself!" (103); to the social voice of the Ladies' Auxiliary member, "Well, here we are again right back where we started. Thank you too, Mrs. Clarke, it's been a real pleasure. That's what we're here for—your hostesses. Three of us, taking turns. Have another glass of punch and don't forget we meet Fridays. Yes, I know it's hard when your children are small, my children are small too—but maybe next year, when you're better organized" (34); to the probing questions of journalist Dan Furby: "You said something a minute ago, Harry, that he made you see yourself and he also made you see it wasn't going to work. What did you mean by that?" (87) to the salacious remarks of old Harry himself, "A lot of stories, Doc, that you used to have a pretty good way of fiddling round yourself. Horny old bastard, still shows all over you. I could name two—" (9). Rhythm, intonation, and diction are varied to suit the individual speaker.

Interior monologues fill in some of the gaps in the portrayal of Doc Hunter and Upward. Here too, the voices are individuated, ranging from the sonorous tones of Reverend Mr. Grimble confessing his despair to Dunc's guilty reminiscences of childhood days with Nick and Benny to Sarah's sharply perceptive remembrances of her long ago school days.

With there being no narrative outside of direct speech, the

speakers themselves must be identified by their manner of speaking
and through their being addressed by others. Interior monologues
are identifiable by the seemingly casual inclusion of some remark
early in the monologue that reveals the speaker; monologues are
linked to dialogues by subject matter. In Mauriac's *Dîner en Ville*,
two characters simultaneously and without any exterior dialogue
recalled the same incident: Ross uses a somewhat similar technique
when one character talks about an incident from the past while
another simultaneously reminisces about the same incident. For example, Caroline Gillespie recalls her first meeting with Nick Miller
while she was visiting Dunc at a Canadian Army hospital in
England. At the same time Dunc in an interior monologue recalls
the same incident. Such repetition of an incident from different
viewpoints is analogous to the musical repetition of themes by
different instruments and contributes to the impression of
simultaneity with which different conversations and reflections,
although perforce read consecutively, can be seen to have taken
place simultaneously. Pauses and interruptions are perfectly timed,
scenes are carefully juxtaposed, monologues are interposed—all
contributing to Ross's carefully contrived pattern. Seemingly in-
consequential conversation renders personality and reveals underlying tensions, attitudes, preoccupations, and antagonisms.

As with leitmotifs in music, words and phrases recur. Characters
are linked by their references to others who are not there—Nick,
Edith, Ida. Objects call up certain individuals; for example, comment on the piano brings up the memory of Edith Hunter; Nick is
defined by his thick boots and fur cap which set him apart from the
other boys who call him "Hunky"; Benny is set apart by his bow tie
and boater; Anna's black handkerchief and red socks both define·
her and set her apart from the other townspeople. Repetition of
descriptive words and phrases has a cumulative effect, recalling
earlier incidents in which the same words or phrases were used,
widening their implications, so that they ultimately operate as "objective correlatives," reverberating in the mind of the reader and
awakening emotional responses. The structure of the novel is that of
a musical composition. Pattern substitutes for plot with the repetition of names, always with the same modifier: "Big Anna," "Nick
the Hunky," "poor Edith"; and the return to the same incident by
different individuals: Edith Hunter playing "Redwing," Big Anna
scrubbing for townswomen, Maisie caring for the sick in her parlor,

Nick being harassed by schoolmates. Much as various themes in music are orchestrated for different instruments—all contribute to the musical cycle.

The movement of the novel can be seen to be centrifugal, beginning at the center and circling outward, expanding to encompass the entire community, past, present, and future. The pivot is "Sawbones" Hunter who has been a participant in the lives of all the townspeople and yet, like most of Ross's central characters, has always remained to some extent an outsider.

Various episodes involving the townspeople past and present are referred to in dialogue and monologue, but are left incomplete; the reader must fill in the gaps. It becomes apparent, for example, although never actually stated, that Doc Hunter had an affair with Ida Robinson, Dunc's grandmother, many years earlier. Several situations introduced in the novel are left unresolved. As we look into the future we expect Caroline to be the stronger partner in her marriage as were the two generations of Gillespie wives before her—Sarah and Ida. But we wonder how satisfactory her life will be—married to a man who is chairman of the hospital board, member of the school board, member of the town council—especially with a good many resentful Upward natives watching her every move. We wonder also how Nick will resolve the problems inherent in his return to his home town. He will have Dunc and Benny and Caroline to support him, but with a number of Upward citizens like Ernie Harp and his wife preparing for the attack, he will certainly have resentment and prejudice to cope with once more. We wonder whether Benny will have the courage to break away from the town and free himself from bitter memories of the past and suspicions of the present, or whether he will give the watchful town an excuse to destroy him. When we put down the novel we realize that we care about those individuals and what happens to them. Through these brief encounters, bits of conversation, an occasional flashback, we have become involved in their lives—their problems, hopes, and dreams.

VI *Themes*

Although ostensibly about Hunter himself, the novel is really concerned with universal human experience: love and sexuality, birth and death, youth and old age.

One major theme of the novel is communication and the failure of communication, the reaching out to another human being and the failure to reach out. As Doc in his farewell speech says:

—one of the things I'll remember, and will probably be puzzling over as long as I'm able to puzzle, is the damfool way you keep spoiling life for yourselves, bringing out the worst in one another. There's so much good here, and you keep throwing it away. . . .
A family doctor sees a lot of what's going on behind the scenes, and one of the things that has always impressed me is the enormous amount of sympathy and goodwill that springs up the moment someone is in trouble. When there's illness or death, the neighbours rush to help. No second thoughts—one question only: what can we do? They look after the children, bring food, wash clothes, sit up at night. I've often seen so much food coming into a house that the family has had to try giving some of it away again before it spoiled. But then the trouble passes, the household gets reorganized, and this little burst of spontaneous kindness, instead of helping to establish new relationships, make the town an easier, happier place to live in, sputters out in the old bitterness and spite. I'm not taking it on myself to lecture you. Your lives are yours, it's all behind me now, but I can't help saying what a pity, what a waste. . . . (130 - 31)

Interwoven with the theme of communication is that of the hypocrisy, pettiness, and prejudice of this small town. Ross reveals the unhappy and at time ruinous effects of Upward's misconceived view of morality on the lives of many of the townspeople; on Nick Miller now returning as town doctor; on Benny Fox, the town musician; on Maisie Bell, the closest thing to a "scarlet woman" Upward has. One citizen remarks of Maisie, "The scarlet by this time must be faded to a pretty pale pink. Fifty-five if she's a day" (20). Not faded enough, however; for although her parlor has been for many years Upward's only nursing home, the town does not invite Maisie to the present celebration: "Ever notice how we've all got a good word for her, but we don't want to be seen in her company." (19). So Maisie is snubbed while Harry, whose "favours for the city fathers" are more undercover, is accepted. The disillusioned minister comments on the superficiality of the town's religious practice: "They sing *Praise God from Whom all blessings flow* with the assurance of the chosen, and there is not one word they understand. They bow their heads for the benediction, but their hearts are closed and dry" (72).

VII   *Conclusion*

Sawbones Memorial is Ross's most technically brilliant novel, successfully incorporating cinematic and musical techniques. By skillful use of time and associational memory Ross involves the reader in the hopes, fears, guilts, prejudices, and dreams of a cross section of humanity. Upward becomes a microcosm of the world, through which the writer reveals that, although modern life has materially improved (Upward now has a modern hospital and the hardships of the homestead are long past), human nature remains the same; in Doc's and the novel's last words, "Everything else though just about the same." The name of the town is, therefore, ironic. In these few hours in the lives of Upward's townspeople, Ross explores universal aspects of the human condition—with skill and economy interweaving the tragic with the comic, and the sense of waste together with the sense of hope which underlie life in this and any community. Much of the tension of the novel evolves from the contrasting and counterpointing of the two polarities of man's experience: frustration and fulfillment, openness and hypocrisy, meanness and generosity.

CHAPTER 7

Sinclair Ross's Fictional World

Identity, the truest sense of self and tribe, the deepest loyalty to place and way of life, is inescapably local, and it is my faith that all the most serious art and literature came out of that seedbed even though the writer's experience goes far beyond it. Much of the felt life and the observed character and place that give a novel body and authenticity, much of the unconsciously absorbed store of images and ideas, comes ultimately from the shared experience of a community or region. There is a kind of provincialism, minus the aggressiveness and self-consciousness, that encompasses the most profound things that a writer has to say.

— Wallace Stegner[1]

I Saskatchewan

T HE "seedbed" out of which Ross's fiction grows is rural and small-town Saskatchewan. Ross spent his childhood and adolescence on prairie homesteads and farms, and his years from sixteen to twenty-five in small towns. He writes out of his own experience and observation of homesteading, drought, and depression. The dust bowl thirties are generally considered to be Ross's world. Certainly most of his early stories as well as his first novel are located in the bleak prairie of the depression years. Such intense stories as "The Painted Door," "The Lamp at Noon," "A Field of Wheat," and "Not By Rain Alone," dramatize man's struggle with the grim and desperate prairie world of the dust bowl, and explore with compassion and understanding the effect of their struggles on individuals and on human relations. In later works these difficult years, if not actually present, are shown as influencing the earlier, formative life of the protagonist. In *Whir of Gold*, flashback sequences frequently return the action from Montreal to Saskatchewan to reveal the profound effect the 1930's of Sonny McAlpine's childhood had on his development. Both *The Well* and

134

Sawbones Memorial are set in a subsequent time which looks back on the 1930's from the perspective of increased prosperity. In *The Well*, the successful farmer of the 1950's recalls his early struggling years as his happiest and most satisfying. *Sawbones Memorial* looks back from a comfortable 1948 to such challenges of earlier times as homesteading, the depression, the two wars, and the flu epidemic.

II *The Community*

The community which Ross views most harshly is the small prairie town. On the whole, the townspeople themselves are stereotypes: narrow, prejudiced, conventional, suspicious of anyone who because of religion, race, background, or any other sign of individuality fails to fit into the prescribed mold. Through succeeding years and generations these people do not change; they incestuously perpetuate their own limited, suspicious natures in their offspring. Thus Mrs. Finley and Mrs. Wenderby of 1930's Horizon are reincarnated in Mrs. Ernie Harp and her friends in 1948's Upward. The women in particular are those townspeople who most enforce the conventional mores and view with suspicion any deviation from the accepted norm, and every attempt by an outsider—such as Upward's English war bride Caroline Gillespie—to win acceptance. Ross's towns are places to leave if one wishes to be free or successful or creative. Those who stay do so because—like Philip Bentley—they are trapped or perhaps, like Benny Fox afraid to leave. It seems that an outsider such as Doc Hunter may come to the small town and survive. Formed by an exterior reality, he can view the town with an unjaundiced eye and accept its foibles and strictures with honesty and compassion. Caroline Gillespie evinces an even more dangerous attitude for an outsider; her repression, in her desire to be accepted, of her own instinctively rebellious attitude to the town's pettiness suggests that the town may ultimately succeed in distorting her view of reality despite her vitality and eagerness.

The city is viewed somewhat equivocally. Those who see the city most positively are those who have not experienced urban life: for Philip Bentley, Judith West, and old Larson, the city symbolizes freedom and opportunity yet to be attained. For Sonny McAlpine, although the city proves to be lonely and unsympathetic, it retains the potential for fame and fortune. For Benny Fox, whose first urban experience is unpleasant, the city still holds the possibility for a more liberated life. But for Chris Rowe the city is the place from which he is running.

Nature, too, is viewed ambivalently. For the homesteader, nature is the antagonist in a bitter, never ending struggle; yet in retrospect, as Hatty Glenn and later—Larson—realize, nature may unite men and women who, in their joint fight against it, achieve together a satisfaction which later riches cannot replace. Nature can destroy—physically, the way Eleanor in "September Snow" is destroyed; or, more often, psychologically, as Ellen in "The Lamp at Noon" is destroyed. It can drain man's strength and hope, as John in "A Field of Wheat," discovers. But it can also be restorative as Chris Rowe and Philip Bentley find.

III   *Significance of the Past*

From his earliest writing, Ross is much concerned with the influence on the present of the past, and in contrasting past with present, illusion with reality. The protagonist in Ross's first story thinks back twenty years and contrasts the present with a happier, more hope filled past. Philip Bentley carries into adulthood resentment of his mother and a compulsion to emulate his unknown father. Chris Rowe's childhood is shown as the cause of his development into a superficial, amoral young criminal; given the opportunity for a more normal life, he develops into a warmer, more humane person. Most of Ross's troubled farm wives can be explained by the accumulation of years which influence their present actions. Ann in "The Painted Door" capitulates to Steven, not because of one lonely day, but because of seven years of loneliness. Sonny McAlpine's Saskatchewan childhood, juxtaposed with present experiences, creates a tension between past hopes and present realities.

Dreaming is necessary to sustain hope in Ross's world. Few of his characters can find satisfaction in present reality. The illusions of farmers like Paul in "The Lamp at Noon" make reality, which is unbearable for those who, like his wife, have no dream to sustain them, bearable. Farmers dream of a successful harvest, mothers of a better life for their children; children, the most imaginative of all, dream of an improbable future. The conflict of the dream world with reality is most developed in *The Well*, where Larson attempts to find comfort in an illusory world which he cannot find in a reality materially prosperous but spiritually empty.

IV Men and Women

Marriages are rarely satisfactory in Ross's world. Most of his farmers and their wives are at odds with each other because of poverty, incessant work, and a bleak future. Women are dissatisfied with their dreary, isolated existence. Trapped in their houses alone in blizzard or sandstorm, they are more isolated and more helpless against the elements than their husbands. They dream of a better life, and the lack of minor luxuries of dress or dancing or music lessons becomes symbolic of their lost or dying hopes. Bickering and bitter recrimination become their response to their situation. Men reply to their wives' resentment with a stoic endurance, silence, rarely with argument; they grimly persist in their hope for the one successful harvest which will repay their years of dogged labor. Their life is the land. To leave it would for them be an admission of failure, a failure they associate with a loss of their manhood.

Rarely is affection, or even much attempt at communication, evident between husbands and wives. Even Ellen's devoted husband in "The Painted Door" is in his dogged love silent and plodding. Ironically, love leads him to the same exhausting labor on the land as his fellows, so that despite his devotion, he unwittingly and unknowingly creates the same divisiveness between himself and his wife that more overtly divided couples experience. Philip Bentley finds his marriage bearable only by preserving the same dour, grim-lipped silence as Ross's struggling farmers. Whereas they escape from their wives to the barn, he escapes from his wife into his study.

Throughout his fiction Ross explores the problem of human communication. From his first story which recounts the breakdown of a marriage he mourns the absence of compassion, communication, and human sympathy in the world. Doc Hunter's words to the townspeople of Upward, written in 1974, could have been spoken to the Bentleys and their Horizon neighbors forty years earlier, or to the earlier protagonists of Ross's stories: ". . . one of the things I'll remember, and will probably be puzzling over as long as I'm able to puzzle, is the damfool way you keep spoiling life for yourselves, bringing out the worst in one another. There's so much good here, and you keep throwing it away . . ." (130).

Ross's exploration of male-female relationships rarely includes courtship. The one story centering upon youthful romance, "Not by Rain Alone," is fraught with irony. A young girl urges her lover not

to delay their marriage. The reader has been given a picture of the
bleak future awaiting her: the drab and unkempt shack which will
be her home, the infertile, subsistence level soil of the farm, the
girl's own more comfortable background which leaves her ill-
prepared for such a life.

Many of the women come from better backgrounds than their
husbands: Eleanor in "Not By Rain Alone," Ann in "The Painted
Door," Ellen in "The Lamp at Noon." These women are better
educated and generally view their situation more realistically, and
often more practically, than their husbands. Ellen, for example, ad-
vises her husband to grow fibrous crops; but he continues to grow
wheat, with the result that his farm is stripped of its topsoil.

Ross's women are not only better educated and frequently from
more prosperous homes than their husbands, but they are often
seen to demonstrate more initiative. It is Mrs. Bentley, after all,
who attempts to find a way for her husband out of the ministry and
for both of them out of the small prairie town. It is she who suggests
operating a book and music store in the city, and who, in fact,
originally seduced her husband into marriage. The older Sylvia is
the aggressor in her sexual relationship with Chris Rowe. It is she
who plots her husband's death, kills him, and then by sheer strength
of will compels Chris to assist her. It is Mad who picks up Sonny
McAlpine in a nightclub, rather than vice versa, then moves into his
room to look after him, and goes back to her waitressing job to buy
their food. In one fashion or another, these women are domineering, yet loving and maternal in their protectiveness toward their
men—who in many ways take on aspects of sons rather than lovers
or husbands.

V *Alienation*

Ross's protagonists are outsiders. The Bentleys, who struggle to
fulfill at least a modicum of the small town's expectations of the
minister and his wife, obviously do not fit. Even their two friends in
Horizon are outsiders: the teacher who is too outspoken and the
young choir girl who, to the town's consternation, may be seen singing along the railway track in the evenings. Their surrogate son is of
the wrong race and wrong religion. Chris Rowe is a homeless,
alienated young man on the run. Sonny McAlpine is a lonely farm
boy seeking success in the city. Upward's new doctor, Nick Miller,
is separated from the townspeople by race and his parents' social
status.

These individuals do not fit into the community in which they find themselves. Some, of course, do not wish to do so. Certainly, the Bentleys do not wish to belong to Horizon, although for the sake of their livelihood they pretend to accept its values. Nick Miller is returning to Upward only long enough to "lay a few ghosts"; he has no desire to become one of the townspeople. Yet some would like to belong to their community. Chris Rowe gradually comes to discover himself in the rural setting he had first found alien and frightening; Sonny McAlpine wants to belong in the city, and is unwilling to return to small town Saskatchewan.

For Ross, the ultimate outsider, the most alienated of all, is the criminal. Ross has said that he is fascinated by the criminal mind.[2] Two of his novels deal with criminal activities. The central character in *The Well* is a petty thief who moves away from crime when he finds himself in a world with different values; whereas the protagonist of *Whir of Gold* moves temporarily into the sphere of influence of the criminal element. Ross views the criminal as one who lives in a totally different world, so alien that one who has not participated in criminal activity cannot really comprehend it. This view of the criminal is best seen through Sonny McAlpine who, when he tries to discover how he came to commit a robbery, cannot do so; Sonny feels that he has temporarily entered an alien, unreal world and admits, finally, "I, who have made the trip and crossed the border, come back with blank pages" (121).

Ross does not attempt to get into the mind of the most perverse of his criminal figures, the killer in his 1974 story, "The Flowers that Killed Him." He views the man from the outside, revealing only his innocent appearing, often innocuous behaviour, the mask he shows to the world. Only a few odd clues noted by his son lead to a last minute revelation of his evil.

VI *Art and Religion*

In Ross's world art replaces religion as a spiritual and creative force. Protestant Christianity is portrayed as a bastion of narrow-mindedness which plays a major role in upholding the restrictive conventions of the small town. Religion had been diminished to a hollow adherence to forms in which the Christian precepts of charity and compassion are ignored. It is a narrow and puritanical faith, insistent upon hard work, propriety, and genteel piety. Meanness and hypocrisy are omnipresent while generosity of spirit is nowhere evident. Mrs. Bentley, ever aware of the demands of her role as the

minister's wife, finds herself becoming as mean spirited and pretentious as the Ladies' Aid members she derides. In a work thirty-five
years later, the Rev. Mr. Grimble and his wife are replicas of the
kind of minister and spouse Philip and Mrs. Bentley pretended to
be. The major change in the intervening years is that the Church no
longer plays such an evident role in the community; but the
hypocrisy and lack of compassion remain. A similar genteel,
hypocritical Protestantism is portrayed in Ross's stories such as
"Cornet at Night"; in which the young boy and his mother honor
the Sabbath by sitting in their parlor dressed in Sunday clothes,
playing hymns—not for the glory of God, but so that the neighbors
will see that they are observing the proprieties.

The kind of retributive justice which overtakes Ross protagonists
is in keeping with this harsh view of Christianity. The most fitting
demonstration of retribution is seen in "The Runaway," in which
old Luke Taylor dies in a fire with all his fine horses—a direct result
of the dishonest trade of his balky thoroughbreds and his sneering
advice to their unhappy buyer to "build a little fire under him."
Ross's townspeople see that sexual transgressions are punished—Maisie Bell is virtually ostracized by the community. Benny
Fox's mother finds life so unbearable she commits suicide. But,
although Ross condemns this narrow, righteous attitude in the community, he himself provides a harsh punishment for his erring
characters at the hands of some cosmic power. Ellen loses her husband because of one act of infidelity, and must live forever with the
responsibility for his death. Judith West dies in childbirth.

Women are the staunch upholders of religion custom; their concern with their children's religious observance is related to their
concern that they have music lessons, attend school regularly, and
in general enjoy some of the finer things in life, something apart
from the daily drudgery of farm chores. When tempted to join
Charlie in a holdup, Sonny McAlpine remembers his mother's ad-
monitions and recalls also her encouragement of his music lessons
and her hard work which helped him to get his chance as a musician. Yet her attitude to music is as severe and restrictive as her
religious practice. When he was tempted to deviate from his rote-
like practicing, she was quick to admonish him to get back to
serious work. Such moments of self-expression and creativity were
not to be countenanced.

Ross ties the figure of the artist, which is a paradigm for the
struggling imagination, to the problem of the imagination which he

explores through children. He frequently contrasts the highly imaginative child with the adult who, because of lack of stimulus or opportunity, has lost this marvellous gift for transcending reality. Thus Peter Parker's teacher can only interpret his imaginative account of his Saturday afternoon as a lie. Sonny McAlpine's music teacher, like that of young Tommy in "Cornet at Night," insists that he adhere to the metronome in his playing. Philip Coleman helped Tommy see that his desire to burst the bonds imposed by Miss Wiggin's metronome and express himself was positive. But Philip was an outsider. It is from outside the community that encouragement for Ross's artists comes. The mechanical attitude to music, like the rigid adherence to Protestant religious customs, is not conducive to creativity or to an expansive life, but rather contributes to the repressive, claustrophobic atmosphere which pervades community life.

The artist is central to much of Ross's writing, absent from only one of his novels, *The Well*, which Ross himself considers outside the mainstream of his work. Philip Coleman of the 1939 story "Cornet at Night," is an early example. Ross's artists may be painters or musicians, interestingly none are writers. Not surprisingly they are shown as lacking the milieu for development of their talent: the small town and the homestead provide limited opportunities for the development of creative or imaginative faculties—as Philip Bentley, Mrs. Bentley, Judith West, Sonny McAlpine, and Benny Fox discover.

The search for a son, a theme in three of Ross's novels—*As For Me and My House*, *The Well*, and *Sawbones Memorial*—is connected with creativity. In *The Well* the son is to give meaning to life, to continue what his father started. In *Sawbones Memorial* also, the son is to continue his father's work. In *As For Me and My House* he is to provide a stimulus as well as a continuity to his father's artistic dreams. Interestingly, none of the sons in these three novels is born in wedlock; two are illegitimate, one is a stranger, indicating that one must look outside one's own narrow world, beyond the accepted strictures of society, in the search for a promising and creative future. The father-son theme is common to such other mainstream Canadian writers as Hugh MacLennan and Frederick Philip Grove.

The artist figure, too, is a persistent one in modern Canadian fiction; among the best known Canadian fictional artists are David Canaan in Ernest Buckler's *The Mountain and the Valley*, Del Jordan

in Alice Munro's *Lives of Girls and Women*, the unnamed
protagonist in Margaret Atwood's *Surfacing*, Alex MacDonald in
Hugh Hood's *White Figure, White Ground*, Monica Gall in Robertson Davies' *A Mixture of Frailties*, Morag Gunn in Margaret
Laurence's *The Diviners*.

VII   Ross's Ironic Stance

Ross is a religious writer. A major structuring element of his work
is the dilemma of man, who is created by an unknowable God and
born into an inexplicable and indifferent universe. Entrapment
becomes a basic theme of his fiction. Yet, his protagonists, while
they may be in some way or another trapped, are fighters. Ross's
farmers stand stubbornly—if often futilely—against the onslaughts
of nature: Mrs. Bentley fights against an unending corridor of small
towns; Chris Rowe against repetition of the crime which has
trapped him into the life of a fugitive; Sonny McAlpine tries
desperately to break out of his lonely world only to find crime a
greater trap; Nick Miller, who, discovers that he may have escaped
physically—but not spiritually—from the small town, returns to
face it.

Ross's stance is ironic. The basis of every irony is a contrast
between appearance and reality. In Ross's stories, man on the land
is at the mercy of the elements. Thus the stage is set for a number of
forms of irony. It is ironic in "September Snow" that Will fights his
way safely home through the storm to find his wife, supposedly
secure at home, dying because the storm has invaded their house. It
is ironic that Paul in "The Lamp at Noon" comes to an understanding of his wife's situation when it is too late; that Ann in "The
Painted Door" comes to realize how precious her husband is to her
at the very moment he is dying as a result of her betrayal. Ironic
reversal is evident in "One's a Heifer" when the boy arrives home
to find that the heifers he is seeking have returned; therefore what
he and the reader have assumed to be true is revealed to be false,
and an entire series of events must be viewed differently. In *As For
Me and My House*, Mrs. Bentley, unable to recognize that her own
words expose her own weaknesses and errors, is a victim of irony
through self-betrayal.

Structural irony is prevalent in those stories in which the outcome
of events is seen to be the opposite to what might be expected. In
"A Field of Wheat" Martha delights in the magnificent crop of

wheat, walking carefully "placing her feet edgeways between the rows of wheat to avoid trampling and crushing the stalks" (73), as she recalls the sixteen years of struggle and disappointed hopes now finally to be redeemed by this one magnificent harvest. Within minutes hail destroys the entire crop and her hopes with it.

Ross shows us many individuals who are not strong enough to withstand "the implacable blunderings of Nature": Benny Fox's mother, Doc Hunter's wife Edith, Ellen of "The Lamp at Noon" on her isolated farm, Will's young wife Eleanor in "September Snow." Most of the men survive physically, but at the cost of love, emotion, and tenderness.

Ross's protagonists describe themselves as, or indicate by their actions that they are rationalists or agnostics. They share Ross's ironic view of the universe. Mrs. Bentley and Paul Kirby, for example, watching the Partridge Hill farmers praying desperately for rain after years of natural disasters, conclude: "Surely it must be a very great faith that such indifference on the part of its deity cannot weaken—a very great faith or a very foolish one" (84). Mrs. Bentley's "queer, helpless feeling of being lost" in the immensity of the prairie, her view of the town as "a rocky, treacherous island," her sensation that "when we reached the darkness we could topple off"—all are reactions and sensations with metaphysical implications. Besides unconsciously reflecting her awareness of the precariousness of her own marital situation, they are paradigms for the existentialist's view of the individual's and humanity's situation in a vast, uncaring universe, poised on the edge of an abyss.

Through Doc Hunter, who in his conversation with Upward's minister explains the attitude of the rationalist, Ross presents his own interpretation of man's predicament as a finite being in a world in which he can achieve only limited understanding, a world in which, nonetheless, there exist beauty and the possibility for beautiful action. Asked what he thinks of the universe, Doc replies, ". . . nobody up there even aware of us, much less concerned about our fate, nothing working for us but a few traces of intelligence, maybe a little dust and sweat rubbed off from the original contact. But just supposing in spite of everything we could hang on a while, learn to use the intelligence, spread it round—" (128). *Sawbones Memorial* is Ross's most optimistic work thus far, not because it presents a more hopeful view of human nature or of man's place in an uncaring universe, but because in Doc the author portrays man as accepting of and coming to terms with an indifferent and unknowable world. Not using his intelligence and imagination in obsessive self-contemplation as such earlier protagonists as Philip and Mrs. Bentley—and even Sonny do—but looking outward, Doc shares his knowledge and skills with others; he treats others with sympathy, understanding and compassion.

Doc's attitude links him with the earlier rationalists, the Bentleys and Paul Kirby, who, though less able to act effectively, nevertheless share Doc's and Ross's appreciation of man's potential for courageous and compassionate action. Their view of man's situation can be summed up in their explanation of Philip's sketch of a little country schoolhouse: "It stands up lonely and defiant on a landscape like a desert. . . . it's *Humanity in microcosm.* Faith, ideals, reason—all the things that really are humanity—like Paul you feel them there, their stand against the implacable blunderings of Nature—and suddenly like Paul you begin to think poetry, and strive to utter eloquence" (80).

These words of Mrs. Bentley and those of Doc Hunter summarize Ross's world view as revealed through his fiction, his central concern with man's stand "against the implacable blunderings of Nature." It is this perception of man which stirs him as a writer, as it stirred his alter ego, Paul Kirby, to "think poetry, and strive to utter eloquence," and which explains the gentleness and compassion with which he delineates his lonely, alienated men and women. Ross's own art mirrors back his understanding of the function of the artist to give meaning and value to this world and man's place in it, thus transcending imaginatively and intellectually man's predicament in an indifferent universe.

CHAPTER 8

Conclusion

R OSS deals with universal concerns—alienation and loneliness, the everpresentness of the past, the artistic and
imaginative struggle, human compassion, love, and courage. At the
same time, he roots these concerns in a particular and vividly realized place and time—his own fictionalized or mythic prairie. Ross's
powerful stories and novels of the impact of the landscape on the
human spirit and on human relationships are located in the kind of
prairie homestead and prairie town which formed him.

In the most positive sense, then, Ross is a regionalist. The beauty
and violence of the landscape come alive through his writing—a
looming, sometimes serene, sometimes turbulent presence which
imposes itself on events and people, at once backdrop and actor in
the drama. Setting is integral to development of theme and
narrative. Ross's artistic manipulation of landscape includes a two-
way refraction: whereas the individual becomes largely what the
prairie makes him, the prairie itself, which imposes itself on the personality of the individual, becomes for that person what he supposes
it to be. The prairie thus becomes a region of the mind. Through his
art, Philip Bentley demonstrates the process whereby the landscape
becomes a mirror of the individual; his paintings exteriorize his own
emotions and reactions on canvas in terms of the prairie—bleak,
lonely schoolhouses standing courageously against the elements,
horses frozen against a fence, hills and stunted trees pervaded by
the conviction of approaching dissolution. For Mrs. Bentley, the immensity of the prairie mirrors her own and humanity's hopelessly
lost feeling in an indifferent universe. Her terrifying sensation of
being on the edge of a void as she walks over the dust or snow
obscured prairie, a metaphor for the emptiness of her own situation,
becomes by metaphysical extension the eternal void which ultimately all mankind must face.

More than any other Canadian writer, Ross has captured the

145

brutal struggle of the prairie dweller with the land and the elements, and the psychological effects of this struggle: the sense of entrapment; the restrained, unemotional personalities of those who must brace themselves to accept disappointment, poverty, grinding fatigue, disaster; the destructive effect on marriage, on human intercourse of any kind which this way of life engenders. The rigorous puritanism of the religion which mirrors the austerity of the land is, like the rigid discipline of the metronome in the musical lives of the children, both a result of and a contribution to that control, restraint, and discipline which come to color all aspects of life, which are essential if one is to avoid defeat by the brutal onslaughts of nature and those other individuals whose personalities have been molded by this restrictive spirit. For the tragedy and irony reside in the effect on man of these stern, unbending values, which so often distort or destroy the human spirit.

His regionalism places Ross in the mainstream of Canadian literature. The firm rooting of his fiction in a particular time and place is characteristic of such major Canadian writers as Hugh MacLennan, Margaret Laurence, Mordecai Richler, Alice Munro, Ernest Buckler, and Robertson Davies. Margaret Laurence, who writes out of her own background of small town Manitoba, owes much, as she frequently admits, to Sinclair Ross's Horizon. [1]

Ross exposes and explores universal aspects of the human condition through the interaction of character and setting. His lonely, isolated individuals strive to make contact, helplessly watching the gulf widen between themselves and those they are trying to reach—Mrs. Bentley with Philip, later Edith Hunter with Doc, both women trying but failing to reach their husbands with music. Ross, an admirer of Ingmar Bergman,[2] mentioned that he can imagine *As For Me and My House* as a Bergman movie. He shares with Bergman a genius for creating an image of the tragedy and irony of the human condition—the desperate striving for communication, the silent building tension, the awareness of the void beyond.

There's rain again, and I've set a pail out in the middle of the floor to catch the drip. Between the clinks I hear a fretful swish against the windows, and a crushed, steady murmur on the roof. It's getting late, but still he doesn't stir. I think of the things I must say to him, walk across the room, knock at his door, go in and say them—and all the time keep sitting here, my flesh and ears strained, waiting for the little clink of drip.

The lamp is burning dry. As the light contracts, the room becomes enormous, its shadows merging with the night and rain. He won't come out till

I'm in bed long enough to be asleep; yet I can't go leaving things as they are between us now.[3]

Ross's finely crafted stories and novels are frequently and painstakingly rewritten and revised. Metaphoric language and artfully achieved cadence and rhythm contribute to the intensity of his writing. The economy of style which characterizes Ross's prose is achieved largely through metaphor and through a diction both simple and precise, suggestive and resonant. Having grown up on the prairie, Ross demonstrates that the control and discipline integral to life on the prairie can be adapted to the achievement of a controlled art. His taut, economical, rhythmic prose reflects the bleak, spare landscape of the prairie; his metaphoric expression gives voice to the psychic lives of his protagonists through the medium of those very aspects of their surroundings which mold their lives and spirits. The landscape is impressionistically described as it appears to and affects the protagonists.

Dialogue, which is terse and laconic in the stories—and generally so in *As For Me and My House*, where it is filtered through the mind of Mrs. Bentley—becomes more sophisticated in later works. With *Whir of Gold* the diction, intonation, and colloquialisms of each of the three central characters are markedly different and revelatory. In *Sawbones Memorial* dialogue and monologue, which bear the entire burden of the fiction—mood, characterization, overall effect—is carefully crafted to the individual; the reader rarely needs to be told the name of the speaker after he has heard him speak once, so highly individualized are the speech patterns.

Ross uses a dual perspective in several stories centered on children. The first-person narrator is a young boy and the narrative, told retrospectively by the adult looking back, gives the child's viewpoint and at the same time comments upon events from the adult perspective. The narrative voice speaks for the two points of view simultaneously; the reader is made to comprehend the child's sensibility, to experience his thoughts and emotions. At the same time the retrospective voice of the adult provides a framework for the interpretation of these events and for achieving insight into the other characters as well. This complex use of voice is evident in more recent Canadian fiction as well, notably: Margaret Laurence's *A Bird in the House*, Mordecai Richler's *The Street*, and Alice Munro's *Lives of Girls and Women*.

Ross is not a prolific writer. He spends much time rewriting and revising, and has destroyed much that he has written. As a result, his published works to date consist of four novels and eighteen stories. Of these, one novel was completed and another given final revision since his retirement; it may be that his years after retirement will prove to be his most productive in terms of his fiction.

As For Me and My House remains the touchstone against which all Ross's fiction is judged. A rich, complex vision of man's struggle to cope with himself and his world, it retains a central place in Canadian literature. *The Well,* published seventeen years later, proved somewhat disappointing. The texture is thin, narrative less subtle, and the structure of the final section of the novel flawed. With his third novel, *Whir of Gold,* Ross returned to the denser texture, more metaphoric language, and cadenced expression of his earlier works. Manipulation of time and juxtaposition of Montreal and Saskatchewan are skillfully handled. Although the focus becomes somewhat blurred as the criminal act takes over center stage from the relationship of Sonny and Mad, the novel, as an elegiac recollection of an unusual love affair, is more successful than it has been credited with being. Ross's most recent novel, *Sawbones Memorial,* is a tour de force, experimental in form and structure. The central character, at once observer and actor, sage and hero, is wise, humorous, and accepting of the world and mankind as they are. *Sawbones Memorial,* Ross's most positive work thus far, has yet to achieve recognition for the fine and subtle interweaving of detail and innuendo whereby its portrait of the human condition is achieved.

Notes and References

Preface

1. Henry Kreisel, "The Prairie: A State of Mind," *Contexts of Canadian Criticism,* ed. Eli Mandel (Chicago: 1971), p. 256.

Chapter One

1. Unless otherwise noted, remarks and recollections attributed to Sinclair Ross are taken from interviews I had with him in Malaga and Costa del Sol, Spain in March 1977.
2. Roy St. George Stubbs, "Presenting Sinclair Ross," *Saturday Night,* 9 August 1941, p. 17.
3. Sinclair Ross, *Nash's Pall-Mall* (October, 1934), p. 80.
4. "The Outlaw," *The Lamp at Noon and Other Stories* (Toronto, 1968), p. 30.
5. Ross, "On Looking Back," *Mosaic* III, No. 3 (Spring, 1970), 93.
6. Alan Pearson, "Sinclair Ross: Major Novelist with a Banking Past," *The Montrealer,* XLII (March, 1968), 19.
7. Correspondence: Sinclair Ross to L. M., July 18, 1976.
8. Ross, "On Looking Back," p. 94.

Chapter Two

1. Sinclair Ross, *The Lamp at Noon and Other Stories* (Toronto, 1968).
2. *Ibid.,* p. 11.
3. Roy Daniells, introduction to *As For Me and My House,* Sinclair Ross, (Toronto, 1957), p. vi.
4. John Moss, review of *Whir of Gold, Fiddlehead,* No. 90 (Summer, 1971), 127.
5. Laurence Ricou, *Vertical Man/Horizontal World: Man and Landscape in Canadian Prairie Fiction* (Vancouver, 1973), p. 82.
6. Sinclair Ross, "No Other Way," *Nash's Pall-Mall* (October, 1934), p. 80. Page references appear in parenthesis immediately following subsequent quotations from this story.
7. See Sandra Djwa, "No Other Way: Sinclair Ross's Stories and Novels," *Canadian Literature* 47 (Winter, 1971), 49 - 66.
8. Ross, "The Painted Door," *The Lamp at Noon and Other Stories,* p. 118. Page references in parenthesis are from this text.

9. Ross, "The Lamp at Noon," *The Lamp at Noon and Other Stories,* p. 13. Page references in parenthesis are from this text.

10. T. S. Eliot, "Burnt Norton," *Four Quartets* (London, 1949), p. 14, 11. 42 - 43.

11. Ross, "A Day with Pegasus," *Stories from Western Canada,* ed. Rudy Wiebe (Toronto, 1972), p. 109. Page references in parenthesis are from this text.

12. Ross, "Circus in Town," *The Lamp at Noon and Other Stories,* p. 68. Page references in parenthesis are from this text.

13. Ross, "Cornet at Night," *The Lamp at Noon and Other Stories,* p. 40. Page references in parenthesis are from this text.

14. Ross, "Cornet at Night," *Queen's Quarterly* XLVI, No. 4 (Winter, 1939 - 40), 448 - 49.

15. In the revised version, "wheeling away" is changed to "wheeled away and . . ."

16. Ross, "Cornet at Night," *Queen's Quarterly, op. cit.,* p. 451.

17. Mordecai Marcus, "What is an Initiation Story?" *Critical Approaches to Fiction,* ed. Shiv K. Kumar and Keith McKean (New York, 1968), p. 204. In this study of the initiation story Marcus divides initiation stories into three types: "First, some initiations lead only to the threshold of maturity and understanding but do not definitely cross it. Such stories emphasize the shocking effect of experience, and their protagonists tend to be distinctly young. Second, some initiations take their protagonists across a threshold of maturity and understanding but leave them enmeshed in a struggle for certainty. These initiations sometimes involve self-discovery. Third, the most decisive initiations carry their protagonists firmly into maturity and understanding, or at least show them decisively embarked toward maturity. These initiations usually center on self-discovery. For convenience, I will call these types tentative, uncompleted, and decisive initiations" (pp. 204 - 5).

18. Mircea Eliade, *Rites and Symbols of Initiation,* trans. from the French by Willard R. Trask (New York, 1958), p. 3.

19. Ross, "The Outlaw," *The Lamp at Noon and Other Stories,* p. 25. Page references in parenthesis are from this text.

20. The Holy Bible, King James Version, Matthew 4:8 - 9.

21. Leslie Fiedler, "From Redemption to Initiation," *New Leader* 41 (May 26, 1958), 22.

22. Eliade, p. 19.

23. Ross, "One's a Heifer," *The Lamp at Noon and Other Stories,* p. 120. Page references in parenthesis are from this text.

24. Ross, "September Snow," *The Lamp at Noon and Other Stories,* p. 62. Page references in parenthesis are from this text.

25. Ross, "A Field of Wheat," *The Lamp at Noon and Other Stories,* p. 80. Page references in parenthesis are from this text.

26. Margaret Laurence, Introduction to *The Lamp at Noon, op. cit.*, p. 12.

27. Ross, "The Painted Door," *Queen's Quarterly* XLVI, No. 2. (Summer, 1939), 158.

28. Ross, "A Day with Pegasus," *Stories from Western Canada*, ed. Ruby Wiebe (Toronto, 1972), 106 - 18.

29. Ross, "Summer Thunder," *The Lamp at Noon and Other Stories*, p. 59.

Chapter Three

1. Sinclair Ross, *As For Me and My House* (Toronto, 1957), p. 3. Page references in parenthesis are from this edition.

2. Ross, Interview in Spain, March 1977. See also Myrna Kostash, "Discovering Sinclair Ross: It's rather late," *Saturday Night*, XXCVII (July, 1972), 33 - 37. An interview with Ross in Barcelona in which Ross says much the same.

3. Wayne Booth, *Rhetoric of Fiction* (Chicago, 1967), p. 347.

4. See Friedrich Nietzche, *Thus Spoke Zarathustra*, trans. Thomas Common (New York, 1964), p. 59.

5. David Stouck, "The Mirror and the Lamp in Sinclair Ross's *As For Me and My House*," *Mosaic* VII, No. 2 (Winter, 1974), 141 - 50.

6. See W. H. New, "Sinclair Ross's Ambivalent World," *Canadian Literature*, No. 40 (Spring, 1969), 26 - 32.

Chapter Four

1. Sinclair Ross, *The Well* (Toronto, 1958), p. 13. Page numbers in parenthesis are from this edition.

2. See Chapter Two, pp. 25 - 26.

3. In her article, "No Other Way: Sinclair Ross's Stories and Novels," Sandra Djwa points out that "the Canadian hero is concerned basically with maintaining his own integrity within a chosen community" (47). Djwa refers to R. E. Watters' address, "A Quest for National Identity: Canadian Literature vis-à-vis the Literature of Great Britain and the United States," *Proceedings of the Third Congress of the International Comparative Literature Association* (The Hague, 1962), pp. 224 - 41. Watters gives examples from Canadian fiction to demonstrate that "The truly Canadian heroic figure is one who wishes to maintain his own separate identity *within* the social complex, however cramping it seems to be" (237). Watters contrasts this pattern with "a standard pattern in American fiction [which] has been that of the individual caught in an entangling net of circumstances who tries to free himself by taking to the open road in the hope of beginning a new and freer lifee elsewhere" (236). Chris Rowe tried the American way, but discovered that for him freedom and self-expression resided within the small prairie community.

Chapter Five

1. Sinclair Ross, interview in Malaga, Spain, March 1977.
2. Sinclair Ross, *Whir of Gold* (Toronto, 1970), 52. Page numbers in parenthesis are from this edition.
3. Ross, "The Outlaw," p. 25.
4. This incident is recounted in "The Outlaw," p. 31.
5. William Wordsworth, "My Heart Leaps Up When I Behold."
6. Ross, interview in Malaga, Spain, March 1977.

Chapter Six

1. Sinclair Ross, *Sawbones Memorial* (Toronto, 1974), p. 139. Page references in parenthesis are from this edition.
2. Claude Mauriac, *Le Dîner en ville* (Paris: A. Michel, 1959).
3. Correspondence: Sinclair Ross to L.M., July 18, 1976.
4. Claude Mauriac, *Dinner in Town*, trans. by Merloyd Laurence (London, 1963).
5. Vivian Mercier, *The New Novel: From Queneau to Pinget* (New York, 1966). Claude Mauriac is one of the six novelists Mercier includes in this critical study.
6. Claude Mauriac originally titled his tetrology *Le Temps Immobile* (Immobile Time) but finally decided on *Le Dialogue intérieur*, a title giving precedence to a particular technique of interior dialogue which he developed. But the immobilization of time remained one of his major concerns. His next novel after *Dîner en ville*, *La Marquise sortit à cinq heures*, restricts time to one hour and restricts place to a Paris intersection, but many lives intersect at this point. In a later novel he restricts time to two minutes.
7. Correspondence: Sinclair Ross to L.M., July 18, 1976.

Chapter Seven

1. Wallace Stegner, "The Provincial Consciousness," *University of Toronto Quarterly* XLIII, No. 4 (Summer, 1974), 307.
2. Sinclair Ross, interview in Spain, March 1977.

Chapter Eight

1. See, for example, Margaret Laurence's review of Sinclair Ross's *Sawbones Memorial*, "Sinclair Ross Looks at the Prairies, His Time and Place," *The Gazette*, Montreal, 10 March 1974. In this review Laurence says: "My generation owes those writers [Ernest Buckler, Morley Callaghan, Hugh MacLennan, Sinclair Ross] an enormous debt, for it was really they who made Canadian writers—our *own* writing, out of ourselves and our place, not based on British models, not colonial, a living reality. I personally owe Ross a further debt, for it was *As For Me and My House* which taught me

that one could write out of the known background of a small prairie town and that everything that happens anywhere also in some ways happens there."

2. Sinclair Ross, interview in Spain, March 1977.

3. *As For Me and My House*, p. 27.

Selected Bibliography

PRIMARY SOURCES

1. Books

As For Me and My House. New York: Reynal and Hitchcock, 1941. New Canadian Library Edition, N 4. Toronto: McClelland and Stewart, 1957.

The Well. Toronto: Macmillan, 1958.

The Lamp at Noon and Other Stories. New Canadian Library Edition, N 62. Toronto: McClelland and Stewart, 1968.

Whir of Gold. Toronto: McClelland and Stewart, 1970.

Sawbones Memorial. Toronto: McClelland and Stewart, 1974. New Canadian Library Edition, N 145, 1978.

2. Stories (Stories collected in *The Lamp at Noon and Other Stories* are indicated by an asterisk.)

"No Other Way," *Nash's Pall-Mall* (October, 1934), pp. 16, 80 - 82, 84.

° "A Field of Wheat," *Queen's Quarterly* XLII, No. 1 (Spring, 1935), 31 - 42.

° "September Snow," *Queen's Quarterly* XLII, No. 4 (Winter, 1935), 451 - 60.

° "Circus in Town," *Queen's Quarterly* XlIII, No. 4 (Winter, 1936 - 37), 368 - 72.

° "The Lamp at Noon," *Queen's Quarterly* XLV, No. 1 (Spring, 1938), 30´ - 42.

"A Day with Pegasus," *Queen's Quarterly* XLV, No. 2 (Summer, 1938), 141 - 56. Rpt. in *Stories from Western Canada.* Ed. Rudy Wiebe. Toronto: Macmillan, 1972, pp. 106 - 18.

° "The Painted Door," *Queen's Quarterly* XLVI, No. 2 (Summer, 1939), 145 - 68.

° "Coronet at Night," *Queen's Quarterly* XLVI, No. 4 (Winter, 1939 - 40), 431 - 52.

"Nell," *Manitoba Arts Review* II, No. 4 (Winter, 1941), 32 - 40.

° "Not by Rain Alone," *Queen's Quarterly* XLVIII, No. 1 (Spring, 1941), 7 - 16.

° "One's a Heifer." In *Canadian Accent.* Ed. Ralph Gustafson. Harmondsworth (England): Penguin Books, 1944.

"Barrack Room Fiddle Tune," *Manitoba Arts Review* V, No. 4, (Spring, 1947).

"Jug and Bottle," *Queen's Quarterly*, LVI, No. 4, (Winter, 1949 - 50), 500 - 21.

["The Outlaw," *Queen's Quarterly*, LVII, No. 2 (Summer, 1950), 198 - 210.

"Saturday Night," *Queen's Quarterly* LVIII, No. 3 (Autumn, 1951), 387 - 400.

° "The Runaway," *Queen's Quarterly* LIX, No. 3 (Autumn, 1952), 323 - 42.

"Spike," Pierre Villon, trans. *Liberté* (Montreal) XI, No. 2, (Mars - avril, 1969), 181 - 97.

"The Flowers that Killed Him," *Journal of Canadian Fiction* I, No. 3 (Summer, 1972), 5 - 10.

3. Articles

"Montreal and French-Canadian Culture: What they mean to English-Canadian Novelists," *Tamarack Review* XL (Summer, 1966), 46 - 47.

"On Looking Back," *Mosaic* III (Spring, 1970), 93 - 94.

SECONDARY SOURCES

CHAMBERS, ROBERT D. *Sinclair Ross and Ernest Buckler*. Toronto: Copp Clark, 1975. Contains a series of short chapters on the writings of Ross and Buckler. Sees in Ross's later writings a diminishing emphasis on the beauty of human action. The study of Ross ends with *Whir of Gold*.

CUDE, WILFRED. "Beyond Mrs. Bentley: A Study of *As for Me and My House.*" *Journal of Canadian Studies*, VIII, No. 1 (February, 1973), 3 - 18. Mrs. Bentley misunderstands the causes of the breakdown of her marriage. Sees the relationship doomed to failure.

DANIELLS, ROY. "Introduction" to *As For Me and My House*. New Canadian Library Edition, N 4. Toronto: McClelland and Stewart, 1957. Sees Mrs. Bentley as unselfish and forgiving, the ending of the novel triumphant.

DJWA, SANDRA. "No Other Way: Sinclair Ross's Stories and Novels." *Canadian Literature*, No. 47 (Winter, 1971), 49 - 66. The strong streak of determinism in Ross's works is most often kept within a Christian context. The struggle against nature becomes a test of endurance in which only the very strong survive.

————. "False Gods and the True Covenant: Thematic Continuity Between Margaret Laurence and Sinclair Ross." *Journal of Canadian Fiction*, I, No. 4 (1972), 43 - 50. Ross and Laurence share a sense of the ironic discrepancy between the spirit and the letter of the religious dispensation.

FRASER, KEATH. "Futility at the Pump: The Short Stories of Sinclair Ross." *Queen's Quarterly*, LXXVII, No. 1 (Spring, 1970), 72 - 80. Ross's stories of Depression years on the prairie celebrate endurance despite futility.

FRENCH, WILLIAM. "Too Good Too Soon, Ross Remains the Elusive
    Canadian." *The Globe and Mail*, 27 July 1974. Contains some
    biographical information.
HARRISON, DICK. *Unnamed Country: The Struggle for a Canadian Prairie
    Fiction*. The University of Alberta Press, 1977. A wide-ranging study
    which traces the growth of prairie fiction from its beginnings, focusing
    on the impact of inherited culture as well as landscape on man's mind.
    Gives considerable attention to Ross's fiction as important in the
    realistic tradition of prairie writing.
KING, CARLYLE. "Sinclair Ross: A Neglected Saskatchewan Novelist."
    Skylark (official publication of the Saskatchewan English Teachers'
    Association), III, No. 1 (November, 1966).
KOSTASH, MYRNA. "Discovering Sinclair Ross: It's rather late." *Saturday
    Night*, XXCVII (July, 1972), 33 - 37. Interview with Ross in Barcelona,
    Spain.
KREISEL, HENRY. "The Prairie: A State of Mind." *Proceedings and Transac-
    tions of the Royal Society of Canada*. Fourth Series: VI, June, 1968.
    Ottawa: The Royal Society of Canada. Rpt. in *Contexts of Canadian
    Criticism*. Ed. Eli Mandel. Chicago: University of Chicago Press, 1971,
    pp. 254 - 66. Sees man—the giant-conqueror, and man the insignifi-
    cant dwarf always threatened by defeat, as the two polarities of the
    state of mind produced by the sheer physical fact of the prairie.
LAURENCE, MARGARET. "Introduction" to *The Lamp at Noon and Other
    Stories*. New Canadian Library Edition, N62. Toronto: McClelland
    and Stewart, 1968. Looks at style and characterization in the stories.
McCOURT, E. A. *The Canadian West in Fiction*. Toronto: Ryerson, 1949;
    rev. ed. 1970. This early evaluation of Canadian prairie fiction contains
    a brief evaluation of Ross's stories and his first novel.
McMULLEN, LORRAINE. "Introduction" to *Sawbones Memorial*. New Cana-
    dian Library Edition, N145. Toronto: McClelland and Stewart, 1978.
    Examines some of the innovative techniques of this novel.
MOSS, JOHN. *Patterns of Isolation*. Toronto: McClelland and Stewart, 1974.
    In his chapter on *As For Me and My House* views the novel as com-
    plex, prototypically Canadian in its composition of patterns of isolation
    native to Canadian literature; emphasizes the ambiguous presence of
    the narrating consciousness.
NEW, W. H. "Sinclair Ross's Ambivalent World." *Canadian Literature*,
    No. 40 (Spring, 1969), 26 - 32. A study of *As For Me and My House*
    which focuses on the ambivalence of the imagery, the lives of the
    characters, and the nature of their world.
PEARSON, ALAN. "Sinclair Ross: Major Novelist with a Banking Past." *The
    Montrealer*, XLII (March, 1968), 18 - 19. A brief interview with the
    author on the occasion of his retirement.
RICOU, LAURENCE. *Vertical Man/Horizontal World: Man and Landscape in
    Canadian Prairie Fiction*. Vancouver: University of British Columbia

Press, 1973. The chapter on Ross directs attention to Ross's use of landscape as a metaphor for man's inner reality.

STEGNER, WALLACE. "The Provincial Consciousness." *University of Toronto Quarterly*, XLIII, No. 4 (Summer, 1974), 299 - 310. Sees regionalism as a necessary stage in the evolution of a literature.

STEPHENS, DONALD. "Wind, Sun, and Dust." *Canadian Literature*, No. 23 (Winter, 1965), 17 - 24. A study of *As For Me and My House* which deals chiefly with characterization.

STOUCK, DAVID. "The Mirror and the Lamp in Sinclair Ross's *As For Me and My House*." *Mosaic*, VII, 2 (Winter, 1974), 141 - 50. Views the novel as a *Kunstlerroman;* and Mrs. Bentley's role that of reflector.

TALLMAN, WARREN. "Wolf in the Snow." *Canadian Literature*, No. 5 (Summer, 1960), 7 - 20. *Canadian Literature*, No. 6 (Autumn, 1960), 41 - 48. A study of five Canadian novels, including *As For Me and My House*, in which the protagonists struggle against isolation.

Index